A Curious Student's Guide
to the Book of Leviticus

A Curious Student's Guide to the Book of Leviticus

Enduring Life Lessons for the Twenty-First Century

REUVEN TRAVIS

WIPF & STOCK · Eugene, Oregon

A CURIOUS STUDENT'S GUIDE TO THE BOOK OF LEVITICUS
Enduring Life Lessons for the Twenty-First Century

Wipf & Stock
An Imprint of Wipf and Stock Publishers
199 W. 8th Ave., Suite 3
Eugene, OR 97401

www.wipfandstock.com

PAPERBACK ISBN: 978-1-6667-5478-0
HARDCOVER ISBN: 978-1-6667-5479-7
EBOOK ISBN: 978-1-6667-5480-3

02/01/23

In honor of the many curious students
I've taught over the years,
for, as the Talmud (Taanit 7a) tells us,
"I have learned much from my teachers, more from my
colleagues, and most from students."

"Judge a man by his questions rather than by his answers."

—VOLTAIRE

Contents

Preface for Parents and Educators

The idea that Jews were given *taryag* (that is, 613) commandments was put forth by the Talmudic sage Rabbi Simlai based on his careful read of the verse, "Moses charged us with the Teaching [*Torah* in the Hebrew text] as the heritage of the congregation of Jacob."[1] The numerical equivalent of the four Hebrew letters of the word *Torah* (תורה) is 611.[2] By adding to this the two commandments, which all the Jews heard from God Himself at Mount Sinai, we arrive at a total of 613.[3]

To be clear, the Talmudic sages who championed the notion of 613 commandments readily acknowledged that Jewish law has many, many more than this. As they were wont to do, the sages were advancing a particular symbolism by way of the use of this number.[4] Most famously, the sages say that this number is derived

1. Deuteronomy 33:4.

2. Each Hebrew letter has a numeric equivalent. In this case, ת equals 400; ו is six; ר is 200; and ה is 5.

3. The Talmudic sages point out that only the first two of the Ten Commandments are written in the first person, with phrases such as "I am your God who brought you out of the land of Egypt, the house of bondage: You shall have no other gods besides Me." Based on this, they conclude that God Himself spoke only these two. He spoke the rest to Moses, who in turn delivered them to the Jewish people.

4. A Mishnaic textual source, Avot 3:23, makes clear that the use of numerology (termed *gematria* in Aramaic, the lingua franca of the Talmud) of the type employed here dates back at least 2,000 years.

from the 365 negative commandments found in the Torah, corresponding to the days in a solar year, and the 248 positive commandments therein, corresponding to the limbs (including bones, tendons, and sinews) in a person. This reenforced the notion that an individual should serve God with their entire essence.[5]

An obvious corollary to this exercise in numerology is the notion that the Torah's commandments can be categorized. In one way, the commandments that are categorized positively or negatively are easy to grasp, as the Torah is replete with "Thou shall" and "Thou shall not" commands.

There is perhaps another way to categorize them, too. The mishna in Avot[6] suggests light (קלה) and heavy (חמורה). Rabbi Moses Maimonides, among the greatest of Judaism's legal scholars, provides us with a definition of these two terms in his commentary on this mishna. In his view, examples of light commandments are "rejoicing in the holidays and the study of the Holy Tongue," while heavy commandments include "circumcision and slaughtering of the Passover sacrifice." The mishna continues and concludes that, no matter how one defines these two categories, a person should be scrupulous in the observance of both, "for you do not know the reward of *mitzvot* (commandments)."

There is yet another well-known categorization of the Torah's commandments, and these are found in the Torah itself. The verse in Leviticus states, "You shall observe My laws (*chukim*) and faithfully keep My rules (*mishpatim*), that you may live upon the land in security."[7] The Talmudic sages and later biblical commentators are all in agreement that these terms *chukim* and *mishpatim* represent very different types of commandments.

Mishpatim are laws for which we know the reason. Said differently, they make sense to us and include things like the prohibitions against stealing and murder and of taking bribes. These are the type of laws any normal and decent society would enact.

5. Mishna Oholot 1:8.

6. Avot 2:1.

7. Leviticus 25:18.

Had God not commanded them to us, we would certainly have instituted them on our own.[8]

In contrast, *chukim* are those laws for which we seemingly do not know their reasons, such as the prohibition against wearing wool and linen in a single garment and the prohibition against eating pork and shellfish. When it comes to such laws, we are expected to observe them, simply because they are the commands of God, despite the unclear rationale.

As confusing and mystifying as the *mishpatim* may seem, they pale in comparison for the modern reader of the Torah to the sacrificial rites delineated in the book of Leviticus.

It is a bit of an understatement to say that the ancient practices of animal sacrifice have puzzled modern thinkers. Contemporary scholars generally find it difficult to fathom the Torah's sacrificial rites in the context of modernity. As one scholar put it, "Historians, social scientists, and philosophers have grappled with the origins and meanings of sacrifice, approaching the ample and varied evidence for the sanctified slaying of animals by ancient priests and kings as an enigma in need of explanation . . . .the practice of sacrifice has been figured as an emblem of the savageries suppressed, banished, or transcended by the sanitized rationality of the modern, while its ancient critics have been held up as heralds of present-day perspectives on religion, ritual, animals, or food."[9] Still others are even more blunt in their assessment of the rites described in Leviticus: "Sacrificial religious practices, as such, seem to have lost most of their relevance and resonance in the context of modern western societies. Secularization and the decline of institutional religion have rendered them obsolete, dissolving the specific contexts and discourses that made these practices self-evident and meaningful."[10]

Judaism, of course, has always found meaning in the sacrificial rites, called *avodah* (service) in Hebrew. For more than 1,200

---

8. Why God commands us in matters so obvious is beyond the scope of this introduction but is still worth pondering.

9. Reed, "From Sacrifice to the Slaughterhouse," 111–13.

10. Duyndam et al., "Sacrifice in Modernity."

years, beginning with the *Mishkan* (the Tabernacle) in the Sinai wilderness and continuing through both the First and Second Temple periods, animal sacrifice was the principal form of communal service of God for the Jewish people.

At their most basic level, animal sacrifices served two purposes.

First, they were a means for the Jewish people, both communally and individually, to come closer to God. Rabbi Daniel Kirzane provides us a simple analogy to help make the point. He writes:

> Think about donating money—you give up buying something for yourself so that other people can have a better life. You may not know the people you're helping, but you still feel happy anyway; this is because donating money is tzedakah (which means "righteousness"), and it is a holy act. In the Bible, we find this kind of sacrifice in the laws about the priests and their service in the mishkan or Tabernacle. People give up their animals, grain, and money as a way of being holy.[11]

The second purpose of sacrifices involved atonement. They constituted a reliable system by which the Jewish people could restore and maintain their relationship with God when they did sin. In simplest terms, the blood and body of the animal sacrifice were offered up in exchange for the sinner's own body in the hope that God's acceptance of the sacrifice would be in lieu of His extracting punishment from the sinner him or herself.

Importantly, animal sacrifices were not a mere outgrowth of people hoping to appease God when they angered Him. Rather, this remedy, this form of atonement, is provided by God Himself. As one author put it:

> The symbolism of animal sacrifice in the Bible is a concrete expression of God's justice and grace at the same time. It reminded the Israelites of the serious nature of sin, its consequences for the individuals involved, and for the community at large. Ultimately, these sacrifices showed the Israelites how much God wanted to stay in his covenant relationship with them, so they could

11. Kirzane, "Understanding Biblical Sacrifice (Korbanot)."

become the "kingdom of priests" who would reflect God's good nature.[12]

Although there is general agreement among Jewish scholars and rabbis regarding the purpose of the sacrificial rites, there is an important dispute about their rationale between two of Judaism's greatest legal experts: the aforementioned Maimonides and Rabbi Moses Nachmanides.

In the *Guide to the Perplexed*, a work written for a single student who was having difficulties in faith, Maimonides states that the purpose of sacrifice is to eradicate false notions that certain species of animals were deities. By sacrificing to God the very species that the heathens worshipped the Jewish people demonstrate the falsehoods inherent in idolatry. Maimonides explains by writing:

> Scripture tells us, according to the version of Onkelos, that the Egyptians worshipped Aries, and therefore abstained from killing sheep, and held shepherds in contempt. Comp. "Behold we shall sacrifice the abomination of the Egyptians," etc. (Exodus 8:26); "For every shepherd is an abomination to the Egyptians" (Genesis 46:34). Some sects among the Sabeans worshipped demons, and imagined that these assumed the form of goats, and called them therefore "goats" [*se'irim*]. This worship was widespread. Comp. "And they shall no more offer their sacrifices unto demons, after whom they have gone a whoring" (Leviticus 17:7). For this reason, those sects abstained from eating goats' flesh. Most idolaters objected to killing cattle, holding this species of animals in great estimation. Therefore, the people of Hodu [Indians] up to this day do not slaughter cattle even in those countries where other animals are slaughtered. In order to eradicate these false principles, the Law commands us to offer sacrifices only of these three kinds: "Ye shall bring your offering of the cattle [viz.], of the herd and of the flock" (Leviticus 1:2). Thus, the very act which is considered by the heathen as the greatest crime, is the means of approaching God, and obtaining His pardon for our sins. In this manner, evil principles, the diseases

12. "Animal Sacrifice? Really?"

of the human soul, are cured by other principles which
are diametrically opposite.[13]

Nachmanides simply could not countenance this approach. He notes the many instances in the Torah in which individuals offered sacrifices to God, beginning with Cain and Abel,[14] continuing with Noah,[15] and culminating with the sacrifices of the Jewish patriarchs, Abraham, Isaac, and Jacob. For Nachmanides, these sources prove that sacrifices were a fundamental and appropriate manner in which to worship God and not merely a response to external influences on the Jewish people. Nachmanides also goes on to point out that in many places the Torah refers to sacrifices as "a pleasant fragrance to God." If sacrifices were merely a concession to man's weakness, as Maimonides contends, why would God be so pleased with them?

Here we must note that this debate took place long after the destruction of the Second Temple by the Romans in 70 CE, an event that brought about a cessation to all Jewish sacrifices. Even today, both sides have their proponents and advocates. Determining which was correct or which made more sense, even if the debate had taken place during the era of sacrifices, would not have had an impact on the day-to-day conduct of the sacrificial rite in the temple.

We must also acknowledge that the destruction of the Second Temple brought about a convulsive change in Jewish worship. Up to this point in Jewish history, sacrifice had been primary. Prayer was certainly not a new institution, as it was present, at least on a personal level, among the Jews from their earliest history.[16] How-

13. Book III, chapter 46. However, it must be noted that in his legal code, the *Mishneh Torah*, Maimonides adopts a different and contradictory position. There he stresses that sacrifices are one of the "foundations of the world" and that they are *chukim*, which, as we have explained, are laws based on reasons we do not know.

14. Genesis 4:4–5.

15. Genesis 8:20–22.

16. As the Talmud (Berakhot 26b) makes clear: **It was taught** in a *baraita* **in accordance with** the opinion of **Rabbi Yosei, son of Rabbi Ḥanina: Abraham instituted the morning prayer, as it is stated** when Abraham came to

ever, prayer, if used at all, was a secondary and very personalized means of worship among the Jewish people. With the destruction of the Second Temple, prayer was their only form of worship.

The sacrificial rites may have ended abruptly, but their influence on Jewish worship did not. In their codification of the daily prayer services, the Talmudic rabbis firmly linked prayer to sacrifice, a link that remains in place to this day. They write:

> /**And it was taught** in a *baraita* **in accordance with** the opinion of **Rabbi Yehoshua ben Levi** that the laws of prayer are based on the laws of the daily offerings: **Why did** the Rabbis **say** that **the morning prayer** may be recited **until noon? Because,** although the **daily morning offering** is typically brought early in the morning, it may be **sacrificed until noon. And Rabbi Yehuda says:** My opinion, that the morning prayer may be recited **until four hours** into the day, is **because the daily morning offering is sacrificed until four hours. And why did** the Rabbis **say** that **the afternoon prayer** may be recited **until the evening? Because the daily afternoon offering is sacrificed until the evening. Rabbi Yehuda says** that **the afternoon prayer** may be recited only **until the midpoint of the afternoon because,** according to his

look out over Sodom the day after he had prayed on its behalf: "**And Abraham rose early in the morning to the place where he had stood** before the Lord" (Genesis 19:27), **and** from the context as well as the language utilized in the verse, the verb **standing** means **nothing other than prayer,** as this language is used to describe Pinehas' prayer after the plague, **as it is stated: "And Pinehas stood up and prayed** and the plague ended" (Psalms 106:30). Clearly, Abraham was accustomed to stand in prayer in the morning. **Isaac instituted the afternoon prayer, as it is stated: "And Isaac went out to converse [*lasuah*] in the field toward evening"** (Genesis 24:63), **and conversation** means **nothing other than prayer, as it is stated: "A prayer of the afflicted when he is faint and pours out his complaint [*siho*] before the Lord"** (Psalms 102:1). Obviously, Isaac was the first to pray as evening approached, at the time of the afternoon prayer. **Jacob instituted the evening prayer, as it is stated: "And he encountered [*vayifga*] the place and he slept there** for the sun had set" (Genesis 28:11). The word **encounter** means **nothing other than prayer, as it is stated** when God spoke to Jeremiah: "**And you, do not pray on behalf of this nation and do not raise on their behalf song and prayer, and do not encounter [*tifga*] Me** for I do not hear you" (Jeremiah 7:16). Jacob prayed during the evening, after the sun had set.

opinion, **the daily afternoon offering is sacrificed until the midpoint of the afternoon.**

And why did they say that **the evening prayer is not fixed? Because** the burning of the **limbs and fats** of the offerings that were **not consumed** by the fire on the altar **until the evening.** They remained on the altar and were **offered continuously** throughout **the entire night. And why did** the Rabbis **say** that **the additional prayer** may be recited **all day? Because the additional offering is brought** throughout **the entire day.** However, **Rabbi Yehuda says** that **the additional prayer** may be recited **until the seventh hour** of the day, **because the additional offering is sacrificed until the seventh hour.**[17]

The shift to prayer, with its concurrent link to the sacrificial rites, is reflected in the writings of Hosea and has been embraced by Jews over the centuries: "Forgive all guilt and accept what is good; Instead of bulls we will pay [the offering of] our lips."[18]

While the Jewish people for centuries have been using prayer, or as the Sages often referred to it, "the offering of their lips," instead of actual animal sacrifices in their service of God, many Jews have still not forsaken the notion that sacrifices can and will again have a place in their worship.[19] When will this happen? According to those who subscribe to this view it will be during the messianic era when a Third Temple will be built and sacrifices will be

17. Berakhot 26b.

18. Hosea 14:3.

19. This was universally true for all Jews prior to the advent of denominational Judaism. Orthodox Jews continue to include prayers for the reconstruction of the Temple and the restoration of sacrifices in their daily services. They believe that both will occur in the Messianic era. Conservative Judaism disavows the resumption of sacrifices and has thus deleted prayers to that end from its prayer books. Conservative Judaism does, however, believe in the restoration of a Temple in some form and has retained references to that in its prayer books. Reform Judaism and Reconstructionist Judaism disavow all belief in a restoration of a Temple and the resumption of sacrifices. These branches of Judaism believe such rituals represent ancient practices inconsistent with the requirements of modernity and have therefore removed all or virtually all references to them from their prayer books.

restored. However, to what extent and for how long will is unclear. This uncertainty is reflected in various conflicting sources.[20]

Now that we have covered this important background material, allow me to make a few observations that should help maximize the utility of this book as you share it with your children and students.

A significant challenge in teaching children the five books of the Torah is differentiating between the text itself and the accompanying biblical exegesis. This is particularly tricky in Jewish homes and schools where adults often turn to midrash (a form of biblical exegesis developed and employed by ancient Judaic authorities) as a tool for helping children better understand the biblical narrative. Midrash provides us with important insights into and backstories to the text, but students should never conflate it with the Bible itself. The biblical text is the text; midrash is commentary on the text.

When using midrash to make the text more easily understood (whether in the classroom or at home interacting with my own children), I have always been guided by the approach of Rabbi Moshe ben Nachman, the great biblical commentator from the 1200s. In his famous disputation with the apostate Jew Pablo Christiani, Ramban made this observation:

> We possess three genres of literature. The first is the
> Bible or Tanakh, and all of us believe in its words with
> a complete trust. The second is the Talmud, and it is an

20. These include midrashic sources such as Vayikra Rabbah 9:7, Tanchuma Emor 14, and Vayikra Rabbah 9:7, which maintain that most if not all sacrifices will be annulled in the future. In contrast, the prophet Malachi (3:4) declares that "Then the offerings of Judah and Jerusalem shall be pleasing to the LORD as in the days of yore and in the years of old." Maimonides, in The Guide to the Perplexed (III 32) seems to stake out a middle ground of sorts. In explaining why God commanded animal sacrifices to the Jewish people upon their exodus from Egypt, he writes that "it is impossible to go suddenly from one extreme to the other; . . . the custom which was in those days general among all men, and the general mode of worship in which the Israelites were brought up consisted of sacrificing animals in the temples. . . . For this reason, God allowed this kind of service to continue." Yet, he concludes by noting that "the sacrificial system is not the primary object, rather supplications, and prayer [are]."

> exposition of the commandments of the Torah, for the Torah contains 613 commandments. Not a single one of them is left unexplained by the Talmud. We believe in the Talmud with respect to its exposition of the commandments. The third type of book that we possess is the Midrash, and it is like sermons. . . . Concerning this collection, for one who believes it, good. For one who does not believe it, there is no harm.[21]

I have never been one to insist that students see midrashic expositions as accurate historical accounts, nor have I framed midrashic stories as mere parables. How a student chooses to see this literature is up to them. But what cannot be ignored or diminished are the important lessons midrash offers us. It is equally critical that, when learning these stories, students recognize them as midrash and understand that they are not found in the text of the Torah itself. (Throughout this book, when midrash is used to explain the text, it will be identified as such, or it will be referred to as "the rabbinic tradition.")

In addition to understanding how and when midrash is used in this book, readers should also be familiar with the approach I employ for presenting and examining the central stories of Leviticus. In brief, I have opted not to use the system of chapters and verse numbers most students are acquainted with. This division was first made in the Latin Bible, which was published in the thirteenth century, most likely by Stephen Langston.[22] Langston's system was employed in the concordances of the Vulgate, and this in turn gave Rabbi Isaac Nathan[23] the idea for the first Hebrew con-

21. Nahmanides, *Disputation at Barcelona*, para. 39.

22. Stephen Langton was an English cardinal of the Roman Catholic Church and Archbishop of Canterbury from 1207 to his death, in 1228. The dispute between King John of England and Pope Innocent III over his election as archbishop was a major factor in the crisis that produced the Magna Carta in 1215.

23. Rabbi Isaac Nathan ben Kalonymus was a French Jewish philosopher who lived in the fourteenth and fifteenth centuries. In the introduction to his concordance, Rabbi Isaac wrote that he was completely ignorant of the Bible until his fifteenth year. Prior to that time, his studies had been restricted to the Talmud and religious philosophy.

cordance. The citations in this concordance first give the number of the Vulgate chapter and then give the number of the masoretic[24] verse chapter, which remains to this day the standard format of the Hebrew Bible when it is printed and bound as a book.

However, this printed format of the Hebrew Bible is not the one used for ritual purposes. As part of Jewish prayer services on the Sabbath, for example, different portions of the Torah are read each week.[25] These readings are commonly referred to as the weekly *parasha* or *sedra*. The starting and ending points of each parasha have nothing to do with Langston's organizational system. Rather, they reflect the long-standing Masoretic tradition.

Given my background and training as an Orthodox rabbi and Jewish educator, it made sense for me to organize this book Jewishly. That is, according to these weekly parashas. It is a system I know well and am comfortable with. More importantly, these weekly readings, in my opinion, present a more logical flow for the major themes and stories of Leviticus than do the chapter and verse numbers in common usage.[26]

Each chapter of this book will open with a brief overview and synopsis of the weekly Torah reading. This will be followed by a section I have titled "Life Lessons from This Week's Reading," which has the goal of helping young students think more deeply about the text read each week, as opposed to merely memorizing certain incidents from the narrative. Finally, there will be questions for students to think about as they try to incorporate the lessons from each week's reading into their daily lives.

24. In rabbinic Judaism, the Masoretic Text is the authoritative Hebrew and Aramaic text of the Bible. It was copied, edited, and distributed primarily by a group of Jews known as the Masoretes between the seventh and tenth centuries CE.

25. There are fifty-four such weekly portions, which means that a double portion is read on some weeks.

26. Indeed, there are many chapter breaks that interrupt the logical flow of the narrative that the masoretic tradition avoids. See, for example, the end of chapter forty-three and the beginning of chapter forty-four. This is clearly a single narrative—one we will discuss in detail later in this book—and most modern editors would be confounded by the insertion of a new chapter here.

To help parents and educators contextualize what I think of as the "big picture" questions about Leviticus, I have also included a chapter that discusses how and why Leviticus differs from the other books of the Torah.

All translations of biblical verses in this book are from *Tanakh: A New Translation of the Holy Scriptures according to the Traditional Hebrew Text* unless otherwise indicated.[27] This translation is available in the public domain and with a free public license thanks to Sefaria (www.sefaria.org), a nonprofit organization that, in its own words, is dedicated to assembling "a free, living library of Jewish texts."

27. *Tanakh: A New Translation of the Holy Scriptures according to the Traditional Hebrew Text.*

Introduction for the Curious Student

From the time the Jews left Egypt and built the *Mishkan* (Tabernacle) in the Sinai wilderness to the destruction of the Second Temple by the Romans in the year 70 CE, sacrifice was the primary form of worship for the Jewish people. The Talmudic sages had many discussions and debates about why God wanted sacrifices. In the end, the rabbis seem to focus on two main reasons for sacrifices.

First, sacrifices were a way for the Jewish people, both as a nation and as individuals, to come closer to God. By actually sacrificing something, be it animals, grain, or money, the people were giving something real (adults would say "tangible") to God. Of course, God did not "need" their sacrifices, but they allowed the people to feel that they were giving something back to God for all the good He had given to them in their lives.

The second purpose of sacrifices was to give the people a way to make up for their mistakes and their sins (adults would use the word "atonement" to describe this). In other words, sacrifices were a way for the Jewish people to restore their relationship with God when they did sin. And importantly, the Jews did not come up with the idea for animal sacrifices themselves. They based these practices on what they saw while they were enslaved in Egypt. What was different, however, was that these practices would take on the role of atonement, which was outlined by God Himself in the book of Leviticus.

The sacrificial laws we find in Leviticus can be very detailed and very complicated. To help you better understand them, you will find in the following pages some simplified explanations of the how's and the why's of this complex topic. But before we begin with any explanations, perhaps you are already wondering, why do we need to know these laws? After all, it's been nearly 2,000 years since the Jews relied on sacrifice to worship God.

That's a good question. It's a valid question. But the truth is, while sacrifices may be gone, they still influence the way Jews worship God. Here are a few examples:

- Jews pray three times a day. The morning prayer services corresponds to the daily communal sacrifice that was brought each morning in the Temple, just as the afternoon prayer service corresponds to the daily communal sacrifice brought before sunset each day. The nightly prayer service serves as a reminder that the fats and the limbs from the animal sacrifices were burnt all night long in the Temple.

- The hours for beginning each prayer service, that is, how early can one begin and by what time must one finish, match the exact hours that the daily communal sacrifices were brought each morning and afternoon in the Temple.

- The additional prayer services, called *Musaf* in Hebrew, that take place on the Sabbath and the holidays correspond to the special sacrifices that were offered on these days in the Temple.

It is the prophet Hosea who best summarizes the connection between prayer and sacrifice when he said, "Take words with you and return to the LORD. Say to Him: 'Forgive all guilt and accept what is good; Instead of bulls we will pay [the offering of] our lips.'"[1]

These connections between sacrifice and prayer make for a good reason to study the book of Leviticus. Yet Leviticus is more than a handbook on how the sacrifices were to be performed. The book is also packed with important life lessons, ranging from not bearing grudges to being truthful in business. From the

1. Hosea 14:3.

responsibility to care for the poor to the obligation to strive to be "holy" in everyday aspects of one's life (as opposed to limiting this to rituals and religious celebrations).

Throughout Leviticus, the text emphasizes the dignity of human beings (and what this means for our personal interactions with one another). It teaches us that "an eye for an eye" is not true justice and is never to be pursued.

For these and so many other teachings, Leviticus is something you can and ought to study, and that is what this book is for, to help you better understand the important lessons to be found in Leviticus.

That being said, there is a lot about sacrifices in Leviticus, so it makes sense to answer some basic questions about the sacrifices before we begin searching for life lessons in Leviticus.

Why Were Sacrifices Needed?

As we noted above, many people believe that sacrifices were only offered as a way of asking God to forgive a particular sin. A desire to be forgiven was certainly a reason for some to offer sacrifices, but it was not the only reason. Some people brought sacrifices simply to feel closer to God. Others offered sacrifices to thank God and to demonstrate their love and gratitude towards Him. Still others used sacrifices to cleanse themselves of ritual impurity (which does not necessarily have anything to do with sin).

We should be clear about one thing. Sacrifices that were brought seeking forgiveness from God for a particular sin were never seen as a kind of "Get Out of Jail Free" card. It is true that sacrifices could lead to forgiveness for unintentional sins, that is, sins committed because a person forgot that this thing was a sin. (Intentional sins are far more complicated.) But any sacrifice that was brought without the person also doing *teshuva*, that is, repenting, was worthless. Why? Because a sacrifice without repentance was an empty act.

What Could Be Sacrificed?

The most common sacrifices were animal sacrifices, and only five types of animals (all kosher of course) could be offered: oxen, sheep, goats, turtledoves, and pigeons. However, animals could be expensive, and not every person could afford to buy the animal or animals needed for the sacrifice. Recognizing this, God allows poor people who cannot afford an animal sacrifice to offer any type of bird or even grains instead. However, not every sacrifice involving grains reflected a person's financial status. There were some regular and frequently offered sacrifices (known as flour-offerings) that consisted of wheat or barley flour accompanied by olive oil and frankincense.[2] And sometimes, sacrifices involved wine (or even water). These would be poured into specially designed holes in the altar.

Who Brought Sacrifices?

All sacrifices could be brought by both men and women. Even non-Jews could bring certain sacrifices. However, the actual offering of the sacrifices was done by specially trained *kohanim* (men who were descended from Aaron and who served as priests in the *Mishkan* and later in the Temple).

When Were Sacrifices Brought?

Sacrifices could be brought on various occasions and for various reasons. For example, every day, the community was required to offer two lambs. On the Sabbath, additional sacrifices were required, as was the case of *Rosh Chodesh* (the first day of each Hebrew month[3]) and the holidays.

2. Frankincense is a kind of spice that comes from the trunk of the Boswellia tree. People today use it as a fragrance in soaps, lotions, and perfumes.

3. The Hebrew calendar is a lunar calendar, which means the Hebrew year is only 354 days long (compared to our solar year, which has 365 days). The use of a lunar calendar was commanded by God (it was actually the first commandment to the Jewish people upon their exodus from Egypt.) It is still used

Individuals were also required at times to bring sacrifices, either as atonement for a sin or to enable the person to eat sacred foods (be they grains that were tithed or meat from certain sacrifices). Other required private sacrifices include the lamb used at the Passover seder and calves that were the firstborn of their mothers.

Where Were Sacrifices Brought?

Once the Holy Temple was built, sacrifices could only be brought on the Temple Mount in Jerusalem, and it was forbidden to bring sacrifices anywhere else. This prohibition is still in effect today.

Feeling a Bit Overwhelmed by All This?

If so, that's to be expected. There's a lot of detail here, and it's hard to keep the facts straight, especially because sacrifices are no longer part of our daily service to God. Nevertheless, the book of Leviticus and the many laws about sacrifices it contains still offer us important life lessons that continue to be relevant in our daily lives. So, let's get started and see what Leviticus has to say to us today!

---

today for Jewish religious observance and as an official calendar of the State of Israel. It determines the dates for Jewish holidays and the appropriate public reading of Torah portions, *yahrzeits* (dates to commemorate the death of a relative), and daily Psalm readings, among many ceremonial uses.

Vayikra

(Leviticus 1:1—5:26)

Summary of This Week's Reading

As you may recall, much of the second part of the book of Exodus describes the construction of the Mishkan (Tabernacle). There are no instructions about how to use the Mishkan, only how to build it. The book of Leviticus comes to teach us about the services and sacrifices offered in the Mishkan.

This week's portion gives us a description of the various sacrifices—animal, bird, and meal-offerings—offered by the priests in this newly constructed Mishkan (which was disassembled every time the Jews travelled in the wilderness and reassembled whenever they set up camp once again). It opens with God calling out to Moses from the Mishkan to teach him the laws of the elective burnt offering, the Olah sacrifice.

God then teaches Moses the laws of three types of voluntary meal offerings: unbaked flour, baked loaves, and the shallow-fried meal offering. We also have a description of the last type of voluntary meal offerings—the deep-fried meal offering—and the mandatory barley offering brought on the second day of Passover.

Next, we have the laws of the "Peace Offering," the Shlamim sacrifice, including the prohibitions against consuming blood as well as the specific fats that were offered on the altar.

We learn about the "Sin Offering," the Chatat sacrifice, brought by an individual who is guilty of inadvertently committing a sin.

Importantly, this set of laws describes how the specific sin offering brought by an individual depended on his or her financial position: a wealthy person brought a sheep or goat, a person of lesser means brought two birds, and a poor person brought a meal offering.

The last sacrifice discussed in this week's reading is the "Guilt Offering," the Asham Sacrifice.

Life Lessons from *Vayikra*

The sacrificial laws described in the book of Leviticus, starting with this week's parasha, can be complicated and difficult to follow. And while most of the book is devoted to the how's and why's of the sacrifices, there are still life lessons to be found in each weekly parasha.

With this in mind, let's get started.

A Little Letter and a Big Lesson

As you already know, the Torah is a very special book. Not because it is full of mitzvot and stories of our greatest leaders, people like Abraham, Isaac, Jacob, and Moses, as well as Sarah, Rebecca, Rachel, Leah, and Miriam, but because it is the word of God given to the Jewish people.

Think of it this way. The Torah is God's way of speaking to each one of us, and this means that we can find special meaning in every sentence, in every word, and even in every letter it contains. This week's parasha has a very famous example of a little letter teaching us a big lesson!

The first verse of the book of Leviticus tells us that "the Lord called to Moses and spoke to him from the Tent of Meeting." The Hebrew word for "the Lord called," Vayikra, ends with the letter Alef. In every Torah scroll, this final Alef of the word Vayikra is written smaller than all the other letters, as you can see in the photo below.

Don't be fooled into thinking that this little Alef is some sort of mistake. It's not. There are no mistakes in God's divine words or in His written Torah. So, what lesson are we to learn from this Alef that is smaller than all the other letters?

Our Rabbis explain the small Alef this way. Moses was not the only prophet of his time. There was another man, Balaam, who was also a great prophet. Some say he was as great a prophet as Moses, and this was so that the other nations of the world could not complain to God and say: "God, if only we had a prophet as great as Moses, we, too, could be as great as the Jewish people."

When God spoke to Balaam, it was not something that was regularly scheduled. It was by chance, and the Hebrew word for this is very, very similar to the Hebrew word Vayikra. The only difference is that Vayikra ends with an Alef.

Can you guess where this story is going?

Moses, whom the Torah says was "a very humble man, more so than any other man on earth," was embarrassed that God Himself would call out to him. Moses wanted to be treated just like Balaam. God of course did not agree to this, and so Moses asked that God write the word Vayikra with a small Alef so that people might think that he, Moses, was no better than Balaam.

Maybe you know people who are humble. Maybe you are humble, too. But what made Moses's humility so special that the Torah calls him the most humble person who ever lived?

Here's the answer. True humility—the type of humility Moses possessed—isn't just about acknowledging that which you are not, it's also about recognizing that which you are. Moses could just as easily been described as the most courageous or the most compassionate human being of all time. Why does the Torah go out of its way to only mention his humility?

Given the above definition of humility, it becomes clear why. Moses was quite aware of his weaknesses (including having a speech impediment), but at the same time, he also understood that his strengths put him in the position to lead the Jewish people. A lesser person would have either failed to acknowledge his or her weaknesses, or worse yet, would have downplayed the strengths they did possess to avoid greater responsibility.

Moses knew exactly who he was and what he could do. He never claimed to be or tried to be more than that.

> *Think of a leader in your school or synagogue. How does this person show humility? Do you think this is an important quality in a leader?*
>
> *In what ways do you think you are a "little Moses," that is, a person who is humble and understands who you are and what you are capable of doing?*

Being a Leader like Moses

We have seen what Moses (and his insistence on a little Alef) can teach us about being humble. Now let's consider what Moses can teach us about being a leader, and to do this, we need to start at the beginning of his story.

It is strange to think that one of history's greatest leaders was a child of a slave. It is even stranger to think that he almost did not survive. Only due to the ingenuity and bravery of his mother Jochebed and his sister Miriam did Moses live to become the great person he was!

Then the story grows stranger. He is rescued from the river by the daughter of Pharaoh, the very man who made slaves of Moses's people and commanded that all babies like Moses be drowned in the Nile River.

Moses grows up in the house of Pharaoh and lives the life of a prince. You would think he knows nothing about his people, the Hebrews, who are enslaved by Pharaoh, but the story tells us otherwise. His sister Miriam, who was watching over baby Moses to see if he would be saved, bravely approaches Pharoah's daughter when she pulls the baby from the Nile River and convinces her to hire Moses's birth mother to breast feed the child. In this way, Moses not only knew his true mother, but he also knew that he was a Jew, not an Egyptian.

Years pass, and Moses becomes an adult. Knowing that he is a Jew, Moses goes to see his people and the lives they live. He comes across an Egyptian beating a Hebrew. Moses is so angry about how his people are being treated that he kills the Egyptian. Pharaoh orders that Moses be killed, and Moses runs away to Midian.

In Midian, Moses becomes a shepherd, like his ancestors Abraham, Isaac, and Jacob were. He watches over thousands of sheep as they wander the fields. Moses notices that one sheep is missing, and he goes off to look for it, finding it at a distant stream. He waits until the sheep finishes drinking, then he lifts the sheep onto his shoulders and carries it back to the flock. God sees the empathy and care that Moses had for every sheep and realizes that Moses was a man worthy of leading the Jewish people out of Egypt.

Another day while shepherding, Moses sees a burning bush that is not getting consumed by the burning fire, and when he approaches, he hears the voice of God: "Go to Pharaoh and tell him to free my people." Moses is shocked. He thinks: "Who, me? Who am I to go to Pharaoh?" Sensing this, God tells Moses not to be afraid. "I will be with you," says God.

In his humility, Moses argues with God: "I am not fit to go to Pharaoh. I am slow of speech and slow in the tongue." He even tells God: "Please, O Lord, make someone else your agent." God says no and assures him: "Just go. I am with you, and I will tell you what to say."

Think about how ironic this all is. Moses is returning to the same person who issued a death warrant for him to tell him: "Let my people go." But Moses has God's assurance that everything will work out. Moses should feel empowered and ready to go, but he doesn't.

Of course, we know the end of the story. God convinces Moses to go to Pharaoh. Moses goes, but Pharaoh is not easily convinced. In the end, Moses successfully leads the Jewish people out of Egypt and then spends the next forty years successfully leading them in the desert as they make the journey to the Promised Land.

There are many different leadership styles people employ, just as there are many, many books and articles that try to tell us what being a good leader is all about. This is all well and good, but as Jews, we should turn to the Torah to see what it has to say on the topic.

Here is one way to understanding the example Moses sets for us in the Torah about being a leader. It is not the only way to understand everything Moses does and the example he sets for us.

But it is an approach all of us can follow, no matter how young or old we are. And, of course, it involves a story.

A Hasid once asked his Rebbe: "What is a Hasid?"[1] The Rebbe answered that to be a Hasid is to be a lamplighter. What a strange answer. What could this mean?

The Rebbe explained. In the days before electricity, a lamplighter would light candles (or, later, gas streetlights) so people could see and not get lost. And that is why the job of a leader is to be a lamplighter.

According to this story, the job of a leader is to bring the light to every person. A good leader helps his or her followers see clearly, so they know right from wrong. A good leader helps make sure people don't get lost: literally and figuratively.

And if we stop and reflect on the great humility of Moses, we can easily understand why he was such an effective leader and why he was such a successful lamplighter. He never saw himself sharing his own personal "light," but rather he was committed to sharing the light and word of God with his people. This is what made him so successful, not his personal skills or strengths.

> *How does the story of the Hasid connect to Moses and the lost sheep? What are both stories trying to teach us about leadership?*

---

1. The Hasid was a Lubavitcher, and the Rebbe was the fifth Lubavitcher Rebbe, Rebbe Rabbi Sholom Dov Ber.

Tzav

(Leviticus 6:1—8:36)

Summary of This Week's Reading

This week's Torah reading continues describing the various sacrifices offered in the Mishkan—a topic started in last week's reading. This is followed by an account of the seven-day inaugural of the Tabernacle.

The reading begins by describing the mandatory daily removal of ashes from the altar. This was the first order of the day in the Temple service. It continues to discuss the priestly meal offering, brought by the High Priest twice daily, and by every priest on the day he is first inducted into the Temple service. This section of our reading concludes with a discussion of the various parts of the sacrifices (be it meat or the skin of the animal) that the priests were entitled to take from the different offerings.

Next comes a discussion of the Todah, the Thanksgiving Offering, which is brought by an individual who survived a very dangerous event. The events for which one would bring a Torah Offering included serious illnesses, serious accidents, and even the birth of a child (which is those days could be very dangerous for the mother).

The parasha goes on to tell us about those things which would invalidate a sacrifice. (Invalidating a sacrifice means it did not count, and if the person was required to offer this sacrifice, he or she would have to do it again!)

The parasha concludes by telling us about the ceremony the priest underwent to be allowed to work in the Mishkan. In the presence of all the people, Moses dressed Aaron and his sons in special priestly clothing and anointed them, along with the Mishkan and its vessels, with the holy anointing oil.

As part of this ceremony, Moses himself sacrifices a bullock and a ram as burnt offerings. He then sacrifices a second ram, and their fats are burnt on the altar, along with some breads.

This complex ceremony is repeated daily for six more days, and during this seven-day inaugural, Aaron and his sons are not allowed to leave the Mishkan.

Life Lessons from *Tzav*

A major focus of this week's reading is the Todah, the Thanksgiving Offering, which means our life lessons will focus on giving thanks and gratitude.

The Hebrew term for this is *Hakarat Hatov*. But *Hakarat Hatov* is bigger than gratitude, even though it does touch on the idea of giving thanks. At its core, *Hakarat Hatov* is recognizing the things we have and the people we sometimes take for granted.

A short text from the Talmud, plus a couple of real-life stories, will illustrate what this really means.

The Good Guest

The Talmud often has a way of explaining difficult concepts with simple examples. *Hakarat Hatov* can be hard for some people to fully understand, but a comparison between a good guest and a bad guest tells us all we need to know about being thankful and showing gratitude to others.

> Ben Zoma used to say: What does a good guest say? "How much trouble my host goes through for me. How much meat he has offered. How much wine he has set before me. How many cakes he has brought before me. And all of this trouble he went through for me." But an inconsiderate guest, what does he say? "What trouble has my host gone through? I have eaten one piece of bread

and a single piece of meat. I have had but one cup of wine. All the trouble the host has gone to has been only for his family."[1]

If you go through live thinking and acting like the good guest, you will have few problems showing *Hakarat Hatov* to others.

Describe in your own words how these two types of guest differ from one another. Which type of guest does your family usually have over for meals? Can you guess why?

Showing Gratitude to a Garden

Rav Yisrael Gustman grew up in Lithuania in the years prior to World War II. He survived the war, moved to America and then to Israel, and started the Netzach Yisrael Yeshiva in Jerusalem, where he served as its head until his passing in 1991.

At the Yeshiva, Rav Gustman had a small garden outside his office, and every day he would go out to the garden and water the plants. The students at the Yeshiva would gaze at this action with curiosity and wonder why their great scholarly dean would spend his precious time taking care of plants. Once, upon seeing the curiosity of his students, he explained to them that this was an act of *Hakarat Hatov*—recognizing and showing gratitude.

Here's why.

One day, prior to the war, Rav Gustman was taking a walk with his teacher Rav Chaim Ozer Grodzinski. This was something they frequently did on Sabbath afternoons. Rav Chaim pointed out

1. Brachot 58a.

to him which vegetation and grasses were edible. This information turned out to be very important to Rav Gustman because it enabled him to save his life during his escapes into the forest when the Nazis invaded his town in Lithuania. Consequently, Rav Gustman felt that watering the plants was an act of *Hakarat Hatov* to these various grasses and vegetation that had kept him alive during the war.

So committed was Rav Gustman to this idea of *Hakarat Hatov* that he, the head of the Yeshiva, would regularly perform the simple task of watering his garden while the students were busy with their Torah studies. We see from this just how important the commandment of *Hakarat Hatov* really is.

Hakarat Hatov Activity

(for home or for school)

Use a whiteboard, sticky notes, or even washable paint on a window. Brainstorm with your parents or classmates and write out a list of all of the things that you're grateful for.

Need help getting started? Here are some prompts you might find useful:

- What food are you most grateful for?
- What sound are you grateful for today?
- What memory are you grateful for?
- What book are you most grateful for?
- What place are you most grateful for?
- What holiday are you grateful for?
- What season are you grateful for?
- What song are you most grateful for?
- What story are you grateful for?
- What tradition are you grateful for?

- What moment this week are you grateful for?

- What friend are you grateful for today?

- What family member are you grateful for today?

Even a String Can Teach Us about *Hakarat Hatov*

Itzhak Perlman is one of the greatest violinists in the world today. Over the course of his distinguished career, he has been awarded sixteen Grammy Awards, a Grammy Lifetime Achievement Award, and four Emmy Awards.

There is a story—maybe an urban legend, but full of truth nonetheless—concerning him.[2] One evening, Perlman was in New York to give a concert. As a child he had been stricken with polio and so getting on stage is no small feat for him. He wears braces on both legs and walks with two crutches. Perlman crosses the stage painfully slowly, until he reaches the chair in which he seats himself to play.

As soon as he appeared on stage that night, the audience applauded and then waited respectfully as he made his way slowly across the stage to his chair. He took his seat, signaled to the conductor, and began to play.

No sooner had he finished the first few bars than one of the strings on his violin snapped. The sound was very loud, almost

like a gunshot. At that point, Perlman was close enough to the beginning of the piece that it would have been reasonable to have brought the concert to a halt so he could replace the string and the start over again. But that's not what he did. He

2. Morinis, "Reading for Gratitude."

waited a moment and then signaled the conductor to pick up just where they had left off.

Perlman now had only three strings with which to play his soloist part. He was able to find some of the missing notes on adjoining strings, but where that wasn't possible, he had to rearrange the music on the spot in his head so that it all still held together.

He played with passion and artistry, spontaneously rearranging the symphony right through to the end. When he finally rested his bow, the audience sat for a moment in stunned silence. And then they rose to their feet and cheered wildly. They knew they had witnessed an extraordinary display of human skill and ingenuity.

Perlman raised his bow to signal for quiet. "You know," he said, "sometimes it is the artist's task to find out how much beautiful music you can still make with what you have left."

In a sense, this is what *Hakarat Hatov* is all about: being appreciative for what you have, even if it's not much, and then making what you have good and beautiful and productive. By doing so, you are not showing *Hakarat Hatov* for a specific thing or person, but rather for the life God has blessed you with!

> *Make a list of three things that make you feel grateful for the life you have. Why did you choose each item? How does each make you feel grateful?*

Shemini

(Leviticus 9:1—11:47)

Summary of This Week's Reading

This week's reading, Shemini, is a continuation of the previous week's reading, Tzav, where we learned about the Mishkan's seven-day inaugural ceremony.

The parasha opens on the eighth day, when God's presence descends upon the Mishkan. Moses gathers all the Jews together to witness the Divine presence in the form of clouds of glory descend upon the Mishkan on that day. Aaron offers various sacrifices in preparation for this revelation.

After concluding the offering of all the sacrifices, Aaron blesses the people with the priestly blessing. Moses and Aaron bless the Jewish people that God's presence dwell in their handiwork, and, indeed, the Divine presence visibly descends upon the Mishkan.

At this point, a heavenly fire appears and consumes the offerings on the altar. Aaron's eldest two sons, Nadab and Avihu, bring an incense offering they were NOT commanded to bring, and a heavenly fire envelops them. (While the text tells us that they died because they offered this sacrifice on their own, there is much more to discuss about this.)

What is Aaron to do? He is understandably very sad about the deaths of his sons. Yet, he and his two remaining sons have an obligation to continue serving in the Mishkan on behalf of the Jewish nation. He is unsure what to do, and so he turns to Moses, who shares with him God's command that he and his remaining two sons may not interrupt their priestly duties to observe the traditional laws of mourning. (There is an important discussion to be had here about a person's obligations to his family and to his people and how one decides which comes first.)

The portion concludes with a discussion about the laws of kashrut. Specifically, God explains to Moses, who in turn explains to the Jewish people, how to distinguish between kosher and non-kosher animals. Kosher animals must chew their cud and have split hooves. The Torah lists four animals that have only one of these attributes, but not both, and are therefore non-kosher. We also learn that kosher fish must have fins and scales. Lastly, the Torah gives two lists: species of non-kosher birds and species of kosher locusts.

Life Lessons from *Shemini*

The week's parasha is very much about rules. We learn about the rules of kosher animals (rules which many Jews around the world follow to this day), and we have a story about Aaron's two sons who choose not to follow the rules God gave them.

Kashrut in a Nutshell

Did you ever stop and think about how important certain foods are in many of the Bible's most famous stories? A great example can be found in the story of Adam and Eve. The first and only commandment they are given involves food (not to eat the fruit from the Tree of Knowledge of Good and Evil).[1]

In this week's Torah reading, we have the Jewish dietary laws, which are all about the importance of food in our service of God. Observing these laws (or, as it is most often referred to, keeping

---

1. Despite the many illustrations and paintings that have been done over the years showing this tree to be an apple tree, it most certainly was *not* an apple tree. Most Jewish sources believe it was a fig tree. Why? Because when Adam and Eve first realize that they need something to cover up their nakedness, they grab the closest thing to them—fig leaves!

kosher) has long been one of the things that defines Jews and sets them apart from other nations of the world. It is certainly one of the best known and traditionally one of the most important rituals Jews observe.

The Hebrew word *kosher* literally means "fit or proper." But we use this word to tell us whether a certain food or drink is permitted according to Jewish law. Let's take a brief look as these laws as we try to discover what life lesson they have to offer us.

- **Meat**

  The Torah says that Jews are only allowed to eat meat from certain animals, and there are very strict laws concerning how the animal should be killed and what happens afterwards. As for red meat, the animals must have split hooves and chew their cud.[2] These are animals like goats, sheep, cattle, and deer. Plus, Jews are only allowed to eat these animals if they have been killed as part of the ritual process called *shechita* (more on that below).

- **Preparing Kosher Meat**

  Jews are only allowed to eat meat from animals that been killed by *shechita*—a quick cut to the neck by a super-sharp knife—which Jews believe to be the most painless means of killing the animal.[3] Meat that comes from animals not slaughtered by *shechita* is called "*treif*."[4]

  The man who performs the *shechita* is called a *shochet* (which is the Hebrew word

---

2. When animals (such as cows or sheep) chew their cud, they slowly chew their partly digested food over and over again in their mouths before finally swallowing it.

3. Poultry (chicken, turkey, duck, etc.) must also be prepared by *shechita*.

4. While the word *treif* originally applied only to animals, today, it is used today to describe any food or beverage that is not kosher.

for butcher). The *shochet* works under the supervision of a special rabbi who ensures that he carefully complies with Jewish law when preparing and slaughtering the animals. After *shechita*, the animal must be checked carefully to make sure it doesn't have any damages or wounds, which according to Jewish law would make it unkosher.

- **Why Don't Jews Mix Meat And Milk?**
  The laws concerning milk and meat are strict, and people who keep kosher are careful about them. They have separate dishes, cutlery and other cooking utensils, separate sinks, and tablecloths. (Some people even check their pets' food to see if it has any mixture of meat and milk). Food that does not have any meat or milk in it is called "parve." This means that the food can be eaten with either a meat or a milk meal. Examples include fruits, vegetables, and most beverages.

- **Eating Milk After Meat**
  After eating meat, Jews who keep kosher wait a certain amount of time before they eat foods containing milk. Many rabbis say that this waiting period is about six hours (which is thought to be the time necessary for the meat to digest) before eating milk products. Others say one need only wait for three hours, and there are even some who have the custom to wait seventy-two minutes. Jews from different parts of the world and from different backgrounds follow one of these rules and usually never switch among them.

- **Eating Meat After Milk**
  Milk products are digested much faster than meat products, so Jews who keep kosher don't need to wait very long. The custom is to wait half an hour after eating dairy products like hard cheeses before eating meat. Many people also rinse out their mouths with a parve drink (such as water) before eating meat after they have had dairy foods.

- **Fish And Meat**
  Another rule of kashrut (based on a long-standing custom) is not to eat fish and meat together on the same plate. The reason for this is that the rabbis in ancient times believed it was harmful to the body to eat the two together. It's perfectly okay to eat meat immediately after fish, and many families on the Sabbath or holidays will serve fish as an appetizer before having their meat meal.

For all the rules we have explained, there is a very basic question we've yet to answer, and it's this. Why are Jews commanded to keep kosher?

Some modern scholars believe that the Jewish dietary laws are all about eating healthy.[5] They point out that in ancient times, eating pork would often make people sick.[6] But if keeping kosher were only about eating healthy, how are we to understand the requirement that kosher animals must have spilt hoofs and chew their cud? Or the requirement that kosher fish have fins and scales? Or the prohibition against eating a kid boiled in its mother's milk?[7]

5. There is no question that some of the dietary laws have beneficial health effects. For example, the laws regarding kosher slaughter are so sanitary that kosher butchers and slaughterhouses are often exempted from USDA regulations.

6. Today we believe that these people suffered from trichinosis, a disease caused by a microscopic parasite called Trichinella. People could get this disease by eating raw or undercooked meat from animals infected with the parasite. These infected meats would often come from wild game or pork products.

7. Exodus 23:19.

If we are being honest, these requirements—splits hoofs or fins and scales—are strange. Try as we may, we cannot find a logical reason for them. Is the meat from a cow actually better than meat from a pig? Is salmon really preferable to catfish? People who don't keep kosher would say, of course not! And that's exactly the point. Those who observe the Jewish dietary laws are not looking for logical explanations. For them, it is enough that God has commanded them to keep kosher.

There is a special term for laws like keeping kosher that have no easily understood explanation. They are called *chukim*. In English, they are called "non-common sense" laws, and we will discuss the most famous of these types of laws—that of the red heifer—in just a few chapters. What is common to all *chukim* are the lessons they teach us.

Sometimes God gives us laws that make a great deal of sense. For example, no one questions the laws against murder and stealing.[8] Other times, God simply commands us to do certain things. He does not tell us why, and despite our best efforts, we cannot figure out the "why" behind such commandments. But God expects us to follow them anyway. And that's okay, because this reminds us that there are things in life that we humans cannot understand, no matter how badly we wish we could understand them.

Believing in God is not always easy, and when we are asked to do things we don't understand, it can make it even more challenging. But with belief comes trust, and we believe and trust that God only wants the best for us. We may not understand why it's a problem eating cheeseburgers or pork chops or crab salad, but we recognize on some level we cannot understand that this is part of God's plan for us, which means that it's all for the best.

> *Can you think of some things your parents or teachers ask you to do even though you don't understand why they make you do them? How did that make you feel when they asked? Did you feel any differently after you did what they asked?*

8. These laws also have their own special name: *mishpatim*, or "common sense" laws in English.

Simple and Straightforward Rules

The deaths of Aaron's sons Nadav and Avihu is one of the most difficult stories in the entire Torah. The Talmudic sages (as does the midrashic literature) tell us that Nadav and Avihu were great scholars and righteous individuals, which makes it so hard to understand what they could have done to anger God that made Him send a fire from heaven to kill them.[9]

Nadab and Abihu are killed by flames. Print maker: Jacob de Later, Amsterdam, 1728. Rijksmuseum.nl

These rabbinic sources offer several possible suggestions for exactly what Nadav and Avihu did that was so sinful: They were heard to say publicly that they could not wait for Moses and Aaron to die so that they could become leaders of the Jewish people; they ruled on matters of Jewish law in the presence of Moses and Aaron; they never married; they were married but never had children; they offered a sacrifice in the *Mishkan* while they were drunk! None of these sound like the actions of great men, and none of

9. Leviticus 10:2.

these appear (or are even hinted at) in the text itself, which states as follows: "Now Aaron's sons Nadab and Abihu each took his fire pan, put fire in it, and laid incense on it; and they offered before God alien fire, which had not been commanded them."[10]

Don't worry if you're not fully following this. Many adults don't either.

So, how are we to understand this very strange story? One approach in particular echoes what we have seen so far in this week's reading with its emphasis on rules and the importance of following rules.

Nadav and Avihu certainly knew the rules about sacrifices. Which animals could be offered. When and where they could be offered. How the offerings were to be made. Not just because they were great scholars, but because, as Aaron's sons, they served as priests in the *Mishkan*. And yet, they ignored the most important rule of all. Everything that was done in the *Mishkan*, from the way in which it was built to the rituals that took place in it every day, was to be done "as God commanded Moses." This phrase "as God commanded Moses" was repeated again and again during the construction of the *Mishkan*. In fact, in the final Torah reading of the book of Exodus, which records the completion of the *Mishkan* and includes a summary of all its work, this phrase appears eighteen times!

It's not clear how or why Nadav and Avihu ignored this rule. Maybe because they were experienced priests who knew the rituals inside and out, and they thought that they no longer needed to consult with Moses. Perhaps they were also fooled by their accomplishments as scholars, thinking that they were now capable of coming up with new insights into the rituals. But whatever the reason, they decided to bring a new kind of sacrifice (which the Torah describes as a "strange" or "foreign" fire) without consulting Moses.

Who knows? Maybe Moses would have agreed that this new sacrifice was appropriate and should be offered. But we'll never know because they never asked him.[11]

10. Leviticus 10:1.

11. Perhaps it is merely a coincidence (although there are rarely

Adding to our confusion is the harshness of their punishment: death by a heavenly fire. We tend to think that great people should get a second chance. But Judaism disagrees with this notion. The Talmudic sages and later scholars all agree that the greater the person, the more God expects of them. And this means that God judges the mistakes of great people much more carefully and even much more harshly than He does for less great and average people. Therefore, in God's eyes, not asking Moses if their sacrifice was allowed made Nadav and Avihu's mistake unforgiveable.

What life lessons should we take away from this difficult and tragic story?

First, we are not God. It is not our place to be unforgiving of the mistakes of others, especially if these mistakes were unintended or unavailable. We all make mistakes, and just as we hope others will forgive our mistakes, we should be quick to forgive the mistakes of others.

Second, rules matter, even when the rules don't always make sense to us (like the laws of kashrut). Following rules does not mean we can't ask questions about them. After all, the more we understand the rules, the easier they are to follow. But we should never break the rules and then ask questions about why the rules are important. Doing so usually does not go so well.

> *Are you the type of person who will ask questions about rules you don't understand? (Like, when you help set the table for dinner, why must the fork go on the right and the knife on the left? Does it really matter?) Or do you simply follow the rules? Why do you think this is?*

---

coincidences in the Torah), but the numerical value of the Hebrew word for life is eighteen. Had Nadav and Avihu not ignored the rule mentioned eighteen times that everything in the *Mishkan* is to be done "as God commanded Moses," they surely would have lived.

DID YOU HEAR...

Tazria-Metzora

(Leviticus 12:1—15:33)

Summary of This Week's Reading

As you may know, the Torah is divided into fifty-four parshiyot (weekly readings). Since the Jewish people finish reading the entire Torah over the course of the year during their Sabbath morning services,[1] this presents us with a problem. There are only fifty-two weeks in a year!

1. The idea of public Torah readings is an ancient one, and for many centuries, the prevailing custom among Jews worldwide was to read the entire Torah over the course of a year via weekly readings during Sabbath morning services. (This was done by dividing the Torah into fifty-four weekly portions, a division that necessitated reading more than one portion during certain weeks.) However, in the middle of the twentieth century, various congregations in the United States (primarily Conservative ones) that were seeking ways to modernize their prayer services attempted to revive a long-abandoned triennial cycle for public Torah readings. The reintroduction failed for two reasons. First, in the triennial cycle, the weekly reading would have differed from what the rest of the Jewish world was reading. Second, the Simchat Torah celebration that marks the conclusion of one Torah-reading cycle and the beginning of the next would occur only one out of every three years, instead of annually. For these reasons, in 1988, the Committee on Jewish Law and Standards of the Conservative Movement passed a legal responsum that put into practice a new American triennial cycle. This new triennial cycle, rather than dividing the entire Torah into thirds, divides each of the individual fifty-four portions into thirds. A congregation can thus be reading within the same portion as those who follow the annual cycle but will only read one-third of each portion per year. In addition, this pattern enables the congregation to read from Genesis through Deuteronomy each year, providing for an annual celebration of Simchat Torah.

This is why Jews read two *parshiyot* on some weeks and why *Tazria* and *Metzora* are often read together on a single Sabbath.

Tazria continues the discussion of the laws of ritual impurity and purity from previous readings. The purification process a women went through in Biblical times after giving birth is discussed at length.

Most of the *parasha*, however, is devoted to the topic of *tzara'at*, which is a supra-natural skin affliction.[2] (It can also, miraculously, appear on a person's clothing or even on his or her house!)

A person afflicted with *tzara'at* must live alone outside of the camp (or city) until they are healed. If *tzara'at* infects a person's clothing, the spot with *tzara'at* is removed, but if the *tzara'at* spreads or recurs, the entire garment must be burned.

There is a logical connection between the *parshiyot* of *Tazria* and *Metzora* because the word "*metzora*" is used by the Torah to describe a person with a spiritual disease which, like *tzara'at*, makes this person ritually impure. The text of *Metzora* explains how such a person can be made pure again by the *kohen* via a special procedure involving two birds, spring water in an earthen vessel, a piece of cedar wood, a scarlet thread, and a bundle of hyssop.

We also learn that a home can be afflicted with *tzara'at* by the appearance of dark red or green patches on its walls. In a process lasting up to nineteen days, a *kohen* determines if the house can be purified or whether it must be demolished.

Life Lessons from *Tazria-Metzora*

As we've mentioned, these two *parshiyot* are often read together. They are packed with technical details about the various forms of *tzara'at*, which are contracted because of engaging in forbidden

---

2. *Tzara'at* is often and incorrectly translated as leprosy. It is more correctly a general term for any progressive skin disease (a whitening or splotchy bleaching of the skin, scabs, infections, rashes, and so on). For this reason, we will continue to refer to this skin ailment by its Hebrew name, *tzara'at*, instead of the term leprosy.

speech (which we refer to as *lashon hara.*). They also discuss the purification process for one who gets tzara'at.

Learning about this disease can be interesting (but difficult) and always worthwhile. But it is the cause of this disease, *lashon hara*, that is most relevant for us today.

Lashon hara may be a term you have heard before, but maybe you haven't fully understood it. Here is what *lashon hara* is: **any insulting or damaging statement spoken against or about another person.** This would include saying things like, "Joseph, you're really terrible at science." Or telling other students in your class that Sarah still doesn't know how to add or subtract.

Many people mistakenly believe that something must be false or a lie to be *lashon hara*. This is NOT the case. *Lashon hara* is anything that, if publicized, would cause a person physical or monetary harm or would cause him or her anguish or fear.

In other words, even truthful statements that hurt or embarrass another person are considered *lashon hara*.

Returning to our examples above, even if Sarah really doesn't know how to add and subtract, sharing this information with others is *lashon hara* because she will be embarrassed when other students learn this this about her.

There is another important term you need to be familiar with if you are going to fully understand what *lashon hara*. That term is *Rechilut*, which is often translated as "gossiping." (Some English translations of the Torah describe it as "talebearing.") In reality, *Rechilut* is going around telling stories (which are almost always embarrassing or meant to hurt another person) just because. And there is a very important difference between *lashon hara* and *rechilut*.

Lashon hara can sometimes be true. It may have been said with the best of intentions, but, in the end, it hurts or embarrasses someone else. *Rechilut* always is said with the goal of hurting or embarrassing another person. There is no positive goal whatsoever.

The Laws of *Lashon Hara* Simplified

In this book, we use stories or examples to help explain the weekly Torah reading. However, when it comes to *lashon hara*, it's hard to find any good or uplifting stories, because *lashon hara* hurts the people about whom it is spoken. For this reason, we are going to give you a simple summary of the laws of *lashon hara* so that you can be aware of what it is and try to avoid it.

- **How serious is *lashon hara*?**
  The Sages in the Talmud discuss *lashon hara* at length and conclude that it is a terrible thing, worse even than the three cardinal sins of murder, immorality, and idolatry. These Sages even said that one who regularly speaks *lashon hara* is like a person who denies the existence of God. And in response, God says: "I and he cannot live in the same world." (Babylonian Talmud Arakhin 15b).

- **Can I say *lashon hara* so I won't lose money?**
  The short answer is no. You may not engage in *lashon hara* even if keeping quiet means suffering a great financial loss

and even if other people come to think of you as a "dummy" because you lost so much money.

- **Can I say *lashon hara* so I won't be embarrassed?**
  Again, the answer is no. You may not engage in *lashon hara* even if keeping quiet means that you yourself will be embarrassed. For example, let's imagine that you are with a group of friends who are clearly speaking *lashon hara* about someone else. And let's say there is no easy way for you to separate from them. What do you do? You must sit there, quietly, and not join their discussion, even if this makes you seem boring or not cool.

- **But what if it's true?**
  A truthful statement can still be *lashon hara* if spoken for no good reason.[3] Let's try to think of an example of how this works in real life.

  Imagine that your bicycle broke, and you took it to Mr. Smith's Bike Shop to be repaired. It cost you lots of money to fix, and it never worked well because Mr. Smith is a terrible bike repair person. Can you go around telling your friends or write an unsolicited Yelp review about what a terrible job Mr. Smith did? No, you can't, because all you are doing is harming his reputation and possibly harming his business.

  Now, what if one of your friends came to you and said that her bike was broken and that she was looking for a good repair shop. She has heard that you used Mr. Smith to fix your bike, and she wants your opinion. You can certainly tell her the truth about Mr. Smith (while being sure not to exaggerate) because by doing so you are helping her avoid the same problems you had.

- **Are there any cases in which we can speak *lashon hara*?**
  Yes, there are, but this requires great care.

---

3. Only one type of *lashon hara* reflects lies. Speaking lies (slander) is called "*motzi shem ra*"—literally spreading a bad name. It's pretty easy to imagine how lies, and even exaggerations, can unfairly damage someone's reputation.

For example, if you saw someone harming another person, perhaps by theft or damage of property (whether or not the wronged person is aware of the damage or theft), by injury, or by insulting or embarrassing this person, and you know that the offending party has not made amends (either by repaying the theft, repairing the damage, requesting forgiveness, etc.), you may discuss the incident with others in order to help guide the guilty party towards repentance and correcting their ways.

What's really going on here? You telling the truth could harm or embarrass another, but you are only doing so to try and help this person not repeat his or her mistake. Such cases are not always so clear cut, and it is best to discuss these matters with your parents or maybe even one of your teachers before doing anything.

- **Can we "take it back" if we speak *lashon hara*?**
Sadly, you can't. The truth is that the harm done by speech is even worse than the harm done by stealing or by cheating someone financially, because amends can be made for monetary harms, but the harm done by speech can never be repaired.

This point is best illustrated by a well-known Hasidic tale:

A man went about the community telling hateful lies about the rabbi. Later, he realized the wrong he had done, and began to feel very sad about what he had done. He went to the rabbi and begged his forgiveness, saying he would do anything he could to make amends. The rabbi told the man, "Take a feather pillow, cut it open, and scatter the feathers to the winds." The man thought this was a strange request, but it was a simple enough task, and he did it gladly. When he returned to tell the rabbi that he had done it, the rabbi said, "Now, go and gather the feathers. Because you can no more make amends for the damage your words have done than you can recollect the feathers."

Take a minute to think about this story. What did he do wrong? How does the rabbi's advice help the man better understand what he did wrong?

Acharei Mot

(Leviticus 16:1—18:30)

Summary of This Week's Reading

This week's reading begins with a detailed description of the service the High Priest is to perform on Yom Kippur, the Jewish Day of Atonement. This service is unique in that it is the only time all year that the High Priest may enter the Holy of Holies, and even on this holiest day of days, entry into the Holy of Holies must be accompanied by a special service and specific offerings.

There are several very striking parts to this service. For example, the High Priest was only permitted to enter the Holy of Holies while there was a cloud of burning incense that filled the chamber. He also had to wear special white garments that would be used only once and then stored away forever. (The symbolism of the white garments is easily understood. By wearing white, the High Priest takes on the appearance of an angel!) Finally, while offering the day's sacrifices, the High Priest would "confess" on behalf of the entire nation. In doing so, he achieved atonement for all the Jewish people for their sins of the past year.

Another fascinating part of the special Yom Kippur service was the "scapegoat" ceremony. Maybe you've heard someone use the term scapegoat. In our time, this word is often used to describe someone who is blamed or punished for another's faults or actions. When things don't go well, people look for a scapegoat. But in the Yom Kippur service, there was a real goat (two actually). A lottery was used to decide which of the two goats would be offered as a special sacrifice to God. The second would literally become a scapegoat in the following sense. The High Priest would symbolically place the sins of the people upon this goat. As the verse tells us, he would "lay both his hands upon the head of the live goat and confess over it all the iniquities and transgressions of the Israelites, whatever their sins, putting them on the head of the goat."[1] This second goat would then be taken in the wilderness that surrounded ancient Jerusalem and pushed off a rocky cliff.

Once our reading finishes its description of the special Yom Kippur service in the Temple, it instructs us to observe Yom Kippur as a Day of Atonement during which people must not work and must "afflict" themselves.

The idea of "afflicting" yourself as part of a religious ritual is not unique to Judaism. Some religious people can be very literal and very harsh when afflicting themselves.[2] In contrast, the Jewish practice of affliction on Yom Kippur is taken seriously, but not to extremes. Jews "afflict" themselves on Yom Kippur by not eating or drinking and by not wearing leather shoes.

Once it concludes its discussion of Yom Kippur, our reading turns to more general matters related to the general topics of sacrifice (which, as we will see, includes eating meat from the sacrifices) and holiness.

When it comes to sacrifices, Jews are forbidden to offer them anywhere other than the Mishkan (while they are in the wilderness) or the Temple (once it replaces the Mishkan in the time of King Solomon). Jews are also forbidden from eating blood, whether it comes from an animal sacrifice or simply from slaughtering your cows or chickens for your personal consumption. In either case, the blood from the slaughtered animal must be covered with dirt.

Our reading also has some very firm rules for Jews about keeping themselves holy, both as a people and as individuals. As a people,

1. Leviticus 16:21.

2. In Islam, for example, Shia Muslims mark the anniversary of the death of Imam Husayn, the Grandson of Prophet Muhammad, on the Day of Ashura. They do this by hitting themselves on their heads with swords (to the point of making themselves bleed), walking on burning coals, and beating their backs with chains.

the Jews are warned not to follow the wicked and often perverse customs of the Egyptians and Canaanites. As individuals, the Jews are given strict laws about who they can and cannot marry. The Torah frames these laws in terms of personal holiness, as the verse states: "None of you men shall come near anyone of his own flesh to uncover nakedness: I am Hashem."[3] In practical terms, these means that the marriage between a man and his mother, daughter, sister, and certain other relatives is not allowed. So, too, the marriage between a man and the sister of his wife is not allowed during the wife's lifetime (and this is true even after a divorce), nor may a man marry his brother's widow.[4]

These prohibitions seem obvious to us because these laws are generally observed by people all around the world (and not just Jews!) and have been for hundreds of years. But in those days, certain nations allowed marriage to take place between siblings or other close family members. God clearly did not believe such marriages allowed individuals to achieve the level of holiness He expected from the Jewish people. And to make this point even clearer, God warns that engaging in these forbidden relationships will result in the expulsion of the Jewish people from the Land of Israel. Why? Because a land as holy as Israel cannot tolerate immoral behavior.

Life Lessons from *Acharei Mot*

The Yom Kippur rituals described in this week's reading still play an important role in Jewish worship even though it has been nearly two thousand years since those rituals were actually practiced. Reading the Torah's description of these rituals, along with the Talmudic explanations of them, is a central part of Yom Kippur

---

3. Leviticus 18:6.

4. The exception to this rule is if a man dies without fathering any children. In biblical times, the man's widow was given the option of marrying one of the brothers of her deceased husband. If she (or the brother) did not want to marry, a special ceremony called *chalitzah* was held so that everyone knew the marriage did not take place. Today, a widow is never given the option of marrying the brother of her deceased husband. Instead, a *chalitzah* ceremony is always performed.

worship in synagogues across the globe. This should make us think a bit about the importance of ritual in our service to God. Do rituals bring us closer to God? Or do they make our worship predictable, repetitive, and, dare we say it, boring?

Before moving on, take a moment to reflect on what your answers might be.

Now, let's take a look at the pros and con's of rituals as we try to answer these questions. And you'll get to see how your answers compare to the one suggested below.

The Role Rituals Can Play in our Lives

People often associate rituals with religion, and there is good reason to make that association. All religions have rituals that define and differentiate their worship of God from other religions. These range from the lighting of candles and the blessing over wine that take place in Jewish homes on Friday nights to the celebration of communion in Catholic churches on Sunday mornings or the use of prayer mats and facing Mecca in Muslim prayer services. But it is worth pointing out that we Americans are driven and influenced by rituals in many aspects of our lives that have nothing to do with religion. Think about it for a minute. First-day-of-school photos posted to Facebook, proms, graduations, bachelorette parties, honeymoons, retirement parties, memorial concerts, and even sporting events—all of these are ritual events or practices. We use rituals to mark transitions in our lives and to celebrate social ties that build our families and our communities.

Clearly, people think rituals are a good thing, even if they don't stop to reflect on why this is the case. So, it's worth asking, what do we gain from the varying rituals we make a part of our lives? Here are a few obvious benefits.

Rituals can give us a sense of discipline. They help us not forget birthdays or anniversaries. They get us to our prayer services each week, and, with a little luck, they may even help us be on time for the start of services. They also bring our families together for special occasions, both religious and secular. Would we have the discipline to do all of this without our rituals? It's hard to say.

Rituals are often fun, but they can be practical, too. Rituals can reduce our options and thus make it easier to mark occasions. Can you imagine what people would go through without rituals such as cakes for birthdays, flowers for anniversaries, dinner at Grandma's on Friday nights, or the Passover seder at your house? In a sense, rituals can be said to help increase our focus on celebrating and enjoying events, as opposed to merely planning and organizing them. And this also means that rituals can make these events more manageable.

Lastly, rituals bring people together by helping us mark and celebrate events in the same way. It's true that having only one kind of birthday party for all people of all ages would be boring. But it's nice to know that, on Passover for one example, Jews are reading the same story and singing the same songs and eating some of the same food, like matzah and gefilte fish.

From a religious perspective, this just might be the most important role ritual plays in our lives. It means that you can walk into a synagogue in any country and feel a sense of familiarity and comfort, even if you don't know how to ask where the bathroom is in their native tongue. As one contemporary bible scholar put it, "Rituals are a *practice* of the faith that provide the structure for our spiritual lives."[5]

Yet, for all their positives, rituals can make serving God complicated. Performing the same ritual week after week or day after day can become boring. Worse still, it can lead us to simply copy what everyone else is doing instead of thinking about why we are performing this ritual and what we hope to accomplish with it.

5. Enns, "Why Rituals Are Really Really Important."

Said differently, rituals can cause our brains to shut down. They can also take away the freshness and creativity that is sometimes needed to connect with God.

A true understanding of the Yom Kippur ritual gives us some insights into how to overcome these challenges.

There is a striking debate in the Talmud about the essence of Yom Kippur that centered on a basic question: Is there something unique about the day of Yom Kippur that brings atonement and forgiveness from God without any involvement on our part? Is it the combination of the day itself and the special rituals described in this week's reading that makes atonement and forgiveness possible? Or is there more to it?

The consensus among the sages who were engaged in this debate was that the Yom Kippur ritual, for all its awesomeness and its power to move people, was not enough. Without the personal involvement of each person, neither the day nor the ritual would be enough. The great legal scholar Rabbi Moses Maimonides, who wrote his code of Jewish law long after the destruction of the Second Temple, summed it up best:

> At this time, when the Temple is not established and, therefore, no altar to atone for us, there is nothing else left for us but repentance. Repentance atones for all sins. Even one who was an evildoer all his life but repented in the end, not a thing of the wickedness is held out against him, even as it is said: "As for the wickedness of the wicked, he shall not fall thereby in the day that he turns from his wickedness" (Ez. 33.12). Even the Day of Atonement itself atones only for those who did repent, even as it is said: "For on that day shall the priest make an atonement for you" (Lev. 16.30)

Let's ponder this phrase: There is nothing left for us other than repentance. It means it's up to us. Our religious rituals, whether they involve something we do daily or just on the Sabbath or only on Yom Kippur, are important. They are to be kept and observed. We hope they motivate us to act and to reflect on our relationship with God. But in the end, these rituals are not enough. We must do our part. We must seek out God. We must try to be better people. We must strive to make our world a better place.

Going to a synagogue on Yom Kippur and reading about the scapegoat ceremony is important. Perhaps you will even find it moving. But it's just a start to the process, not the endgame. Or, to use an image most of us are familiar with, helium balloons at birthday parties. They're fun and pretty, but once all the helium leaks out, they're just empty bits of rubber.

Rituals are like that, too. Without our personal involvement and contributions, they are just empty symbols. In the end, it's up to you to make them soar.

What is your favorite ritual at school or at synagogue? Why do you like it so much? What keeps it from being boring or repetitive for you?

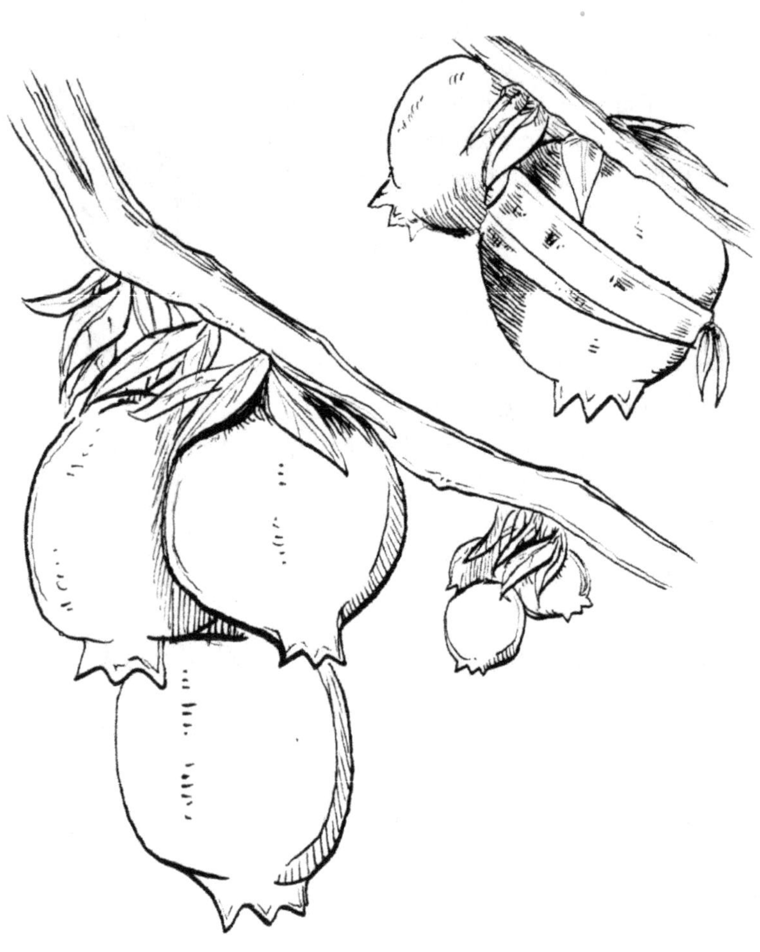

Kedoshim

(Leviticus 19:1—20:2)

Summary of This Week's Reading

This week's reading is a little surprising. As we've seen, much of Leviticus is about the various sacrifices brought in the Mishkan. This reading, however, is not. Instead, it has dozens of commandments, including the gifts one must give to the poor, how one is to love all other Jews, the prohibition against sorcery and witchcraft, and the obligation to be honest in business dealings. These types of commandments are practical and easy to understand. But our reading does not open with any of these. It starts with God's command to the Jewish people to be holy. (We will discuss this commandment below in greater detail).

Our reading then moves on to a long list of commandments that are not necessarily related to one another. But many of them could be said to have some connection to the notion of holiness. This list includes revering parents; observing the Sabbath; prohibitions against idolatry; not lying or cheating (which includes not withholding wages from workers); not to swear falsely or curse; not to mislead others; not to pervert justice, not to gossip; not to be indifferent to another's difficulties; not to hate a fellow Jew, but rather to love every Jew; and, lastly, not to bear grudges or take revenge.

At this point, our reading discusses several interesting and important agricultural laws. We are introduced to the laws of "orlah," which prohibits eating fruit from a new sapling for its first three years.[1] We are further told that the fruits of the fourth year should be brought to Jerusalem where its owner can eat them. If for some reason the farmer cannot bring these fruits to Jerusalem, they must be redeemed for a specially designated amount of money. This redemption allows the farmer to eat the fruits, but the redemption money must then be donated to the Temple.

Other agricultural laws in this week's reading include the obligation to leave certain parts of one's harvest for the poor and the prohibition against planting two different crops in a single field. We are also forbidden to crossbreed animals (for instance, mating a cow and a goat).

Having introduced the idea of prohibited "mixtures," our reading teaches us about the prohibition against wearing a garment made of a mixture of wool and linen (called "shatnez" in Hebrew). The commandment against wearing wool and linen is another well-known example of a chukim, one of those non-common-sense laws.

Back to our list. There are commandments that involve our bodies, like the prohibition against tattoos. Men are also commanded not to destroy the hair at the edges of their scalp or the corners of their beards.

There are commandments that we might today think of as religiously focused, like observing the Sabbath and respecting God's sanctuary, Torah scholars, and the elderly. We are also commanded to love converts.

There are even commandments that involve how people conduct business, like being truthful in one's business dealings by maintaining honest weights and measures.

The list can be harsh. For example, we are told that one who worships Molech (a form of idolatry which required human sacrifices) should be put to death by the Jewish courts. Our reading also describes the punishment which will befall the Jewish people if they neglect to punish Molech worshippers. And as if to make things

---

1. It should be noted that this prohibition goes far beyond just eating the fruit. It also forbidden to feed orlah fruit to animals (wild animals included), sell or give it to a non-Jew, or use it for compost. It is also forbidden to smell orlah fruit, light candles from orlah oil, use orlah-produced cosmetics, paint with orlah dyes, or even use orlah fruit as sukkah decorations.

clearer still, we are instructed not to follow the customs and tradi-tions of the idol worshippers and to be very careful about eating only kosher foods.

Interestingly, our reading ends as it begins, with the decree that we be holy.

Life Lessons from *Kedoshim*

There are so many diverse commandments in this week's reading that choosing just a few to focus on to teach us important life lessons was a challenge. After you've read through the ones below, perhaps you can come up with others of your own!

Creating Holiness in Our Lives

If you were asked, what is holiness, you'd probably have a hard time defining it. Most adults would have problems, too. That's because people can identify things that they think are holy without fully understanding what makes them holy.

Let's use your synagogue as an example.

There are lots of things in a typical synagogue that people think of as holy: the Torah scrolls, prayer books, prayer shawls (called "*tallit*" in Hebrew), even the *mezuzot* on the doorframes of the building.[2] What makes each of these items holy? Is it because they contain Hebrew verses and prayers? Yes. Is it the fact that they are used in

---

2. There is a biblical commandment to "write the words of God on the gates and doorposts of your house" (Deuteronomy 6:9). This is done by affix-ing to each doorframe in a house (except for bathrooms and closets) a piece of parchment, known as a *klaf*, inscribed with specific Hebrew verses from the Torah (the Shema prayer, beginning with the phrase, "Hear, O Israel, the Lord (is) our God, the Lord is One") The parchment is typically placed in a special decorative case before being affixed to the doorframe. The parchment and case are called a *mezuzah*.

prayer services? Yes. Or is it simply a long-standing custom to treat such items as holy? Also, yes.

What's clear is that it's easy for us to think of items used for ritual purposes as holy. But even so, we are left with questions. If ritual items are holy, does that include the special cup we use on Friday nights when blessing the wine? Or the candle sticks we use on Friday nights when lighting Sabbath candles? Or the seder plate we use on Passover? Are these holy, too? Are they as holy as, say, a Torah scroll? Can some things be holier than other things?[3]

Now, let's make this even more confusing.

In this week's reading, God does not command the Jewish people to make ritual items holy. He tells them to make themselves holy. And God's reason for this? Because, as He says, "I, your God, am holy."[4] That's a powerful reason to do something, but this statement offers us no practical advice on how to become holy.

Unlike some religions, Judaism does not believe that certain people are born holy or are automatically holy. Rabbis, for instance, are not holy. They may be well-educated and hard working. They may build great communities and help many people. But having the title of "rabbi" does not bestow holiness upon anyone!

To understand how a person or a people can make themselves holy, we need to look closely at the Hebrew word for holy: *kadosh*. *Kadosh* means that something (or someone) is separated unto and belongs to God, as opposed to things that belong to man. How can people make themselves separate and distinct so that they can belong to God? The Talmudic sages give an interesting answer to this question here:

> **And Rabbi Ḥama, son of Rabbi Ḥanina, says: What is** the meaning of that **which is written: "After the Lord your God shall you walk,** and Him shall you fear, and His commandments shall you keep, and unto His voice shall

---

3. The short answer is "yes." The earliest rabbinic sages, when studying the biblical notions of holiness, quickly understood that there existed a hierarchy of holiness, as evidenced by the various vessels used in the *Mishkan* and by the loftier status of Aaron and his sons compared to the other tribes.

4. Leviticus 19:2.

you hearken, and Him shall you serve, and unto Him shall you cleave" (Deuteronomy 13:5)? **But is it** actually **possible for a person to follow the Divine Presence? But hasn't it already been stated: "For the Lord your God is a devouring fire,** a jealous God" (Deuteronomy 4:24), and one cannot approach fire. He explains: **Rather,** the meaning is **that one should follow the attributes of the Holy One, Blessed be He.** He provides several examples. **Just as He clothes the naked . . . so too,** should **you clothe the naked.** Just as **the Holy One, Blessed be He, visits the sick . . . so too,** should **you visit the sick.** Just as **the Holy One, Blessed be He, consoles mourners . . . so too,** should **you console mourners.** Just as **the Holy One, Blessed be He, buried the dead . . . so too,** should **you bury the dead.**[5]

What are these sages trying to teach us? Simply this. Saying God is holy means that He acts in holy ways. This in turn means that one can become holy by walking in the ways of the Lord. One does this by learning from and copying His actions. Becoming holy is thus a reflection of our actions. By copying God and doing good, not just for us but for others, we give ourselves over to God.

5. Sotah 14a.

It's how we separate ourselves and make ourselves distinct. It's how we make ourselves holy.

Perhaps you noticed something missing from the list above of things we ought to do, which would be to study Torah. Studying the weekly parasha (like you are doing by way of this book) and learning God's laws are important activities. They are so important that the Talmudic sages equate the study of Torah with fulfilling all of God's commandments![6] But study without action is worth very little.[7]

There are no shortcuts for doing good and for making yourself holy. Doing good requires thought and attention. It means doing the right thing over and over until it becomes second nature to you.

A great Hassidic Rebbe[8] once gave some simple advice on how to achieve this. He said, before you act, ask yourself whether God will be pleased with your actions? Not, is this allowed or is this prohibited? But ask will God be pleased with my actions? If the answer is "yes," you'll know you're doing something good and proper, which is one sure path to holiness.

> *Try this experiment. Start asking yourself before you do something, will God be pleased with my actions? Do this for a day or two. Did you act any differently than you would otherwise have? Did you feel any better about your actions?*
>
> *If you're up for a bigger challenge, try doing this for a week and then ask yourself the same questions.*

6. Shabbat 127a.

7. Pirkei Avot 3:12.

8. Rabbi Sholom Noach Berezovsky (August 8, 1911—August 8, 2000), who served as the Slonimer Rebbe from 1981 until his death. A prolific writer, he is widely known for his teachings which are published as a series of books entitled *Nesivos Sholom*.

A Bad Idea Even If It Feels Good

Revenge is a popular theme for authors and screenwriters. Just Google "best revenge movies" or "best revenge stories," and you're search will result in you seeing one list after another. But even in books and movies, revenge is a bad idea that rarely works out in the ways they are planned. The ancient Chinese philosopher Confucius said it best when he purportedly declared, "Before you embark on a journey of revenge, dig two graves." (Confucius did not say so directly, but clearly, he had in mind the person seeking revenge and the target of the revenge. Plans for revenge end badly for all.)

Before we consider what makes revenge so bad (and why God felt a need to command us not to take revenge), we should make clear the difference between bearing a grudge and taking revenge. The following examples will help highlight the differences between the two.

Suppose you wanted to plant a vegetable garden, but you don't have a shovel. So, you ask a friend if you could borrow a shovel. You know your friend has one, but the friend says no without telling you why. A few days later, this same friend asks to borrow a rake from you.

If you were to say, "You may not have lent me your shovel, but I'm a better friend, so you can borrow my rake," you would be showing that you are bearing a grudge. In other words, you did not let your friend's refusal to lend you a shovel keep you from lending a rake to your friend, but it's clear that you have neither forgotten nor forgiven.

If you were to say, "Just as you wouldn't lend me your shovel, I'm not going to lend you my rake," this would be you taking revenge. How so? You are doing to your friend exactly what the friend did to you—denying the request.

Before we move on, take a minute to think about an answer you could give in this example that would not involve bearing a grudge or taking revenge.

Now that we have defined bearing a grudge and taking revenge, let's stop and think carefully about what's involved with revenge. Once we do, it should quickly become obvious why revenge accomplishes nothing other than causing bad feelings between people.

First, despite what people think, revenge doesn't make them feel better. Evidence shows that people who seek revenge instead of forgiving or letting go tend to feel worse in the long run.[9] Revenge seekers are much better off channeling their energy into moving forward positively with their lives.

What's more, revenge might make a person feel worse. Can causing someone else distress or pain ever truly make a person feel better? Not likely. In fact, it's more likely to make them feel guilty, upset, or regretful. And these kinds of feelings tend to stay with a person for a long time.

Of course, it's always possible that a person's plan for revenge could backfire. The revenge seeker might be the one who ends up hurt or in trouble. It's like Gandhi once said, "An eye for an eye only ends up making the whole world blind." In other words, when it comes to revenge, everyone ends up getting hurt in some way.

On a practical level, plotting revenge is really a waste of time. The revenge seeker should ask him or herself, do I really want to waste my time on someone who doesn't deserve it? Better to think of all the fun things you could be doing instead of plotting some wild revenge plan.

9. "Sevens Reasons Why Seeking Revenge Is a Bad Idea."

Lastly, cliché as it may be, two wrongs don't make a right. Seeking revenge won't undo the wrong you felt was done to you. Or, if we return to the idea of being holy, how is it "acting like God" to seek revenge? Better to do the right thing and be the bigger person.

These are some pretty good reasons for a person not to seek revenge. And if revenge seekers were to think clearly and rationally, perhaps then there would have been no need for God to command us not to seek revenge. But people who have been hurt or betrayed tend not to think rationally. Their emotions, be it anger or pain, often get the better of them. To counter these emotions or to help people reign in their emotions, God commands them to not take revenge. He does so with the hope and expectation that their fear of God and their desire to follow His commands is stronger than their hurt and pain.

If only the revenge seeker would pause and ask, "would taking revenge be pleasing to God?", then there would certainly be far fewer revenge stories to find online.

> *If you try to make decisions when you're hurt or angry, are they good decisions? Do you think you'd be better off if you waited a bit in such circumstances before making a decision?*

TISHREI
25 26 27 28 29 30
2 3 4 5 6 7 8
9 10 11 12 13 14 15
16 17 18 19 20 21 22
23 24 25 26 27 28 29

Emor

(Leviticus 21:1—24:23)

Summary of This Week's Reading

This week's reading begins with a discussion about the priests who work in the Mishkan and the high level of ritual purity they must maintain. Doing so requires that they not marry certain women, including those who have been divorced. It also means that they may not encounter a human corpse—except to attend the funeral of a close relative, like a parent, child, sibling, or spouse. The rules are even stricter for the High Priest. He is not even permitted to attend family funerals and may only marry a woman who has never been married before.

We next read about some rules that relate to the day-to-day work done by the priests. We learn about bodily blemishes and ritual impurities that prevent a priest from performing his duties in the Mishkan. There are also rules about who in a priest's family may eat terumah, which is the tithe[1] from various crops harvested by the people which must be given to all priests.

1. The term "tithe" (*maaser* in Hebrew) describes something similar to a tax that the people gave in biblical times to support the priests and the Levites who worked in the Temple. It totaled approximately ten percent of the crops and livestock farmers grew. If it was too difficult to give the actual produce or livestock to the priests, farmers could redeem these for money and then give the money to the priests and Levites. Some people preserve this custom in our times by giving ten percent of their earnings to charity.

Our reading then switches topics and describes which types of blemishes disqualify animals from sacrificial use. The text adds that animals may not be sacrificed before they are eight days old, nor may a mother animal and her offspring be sacrificed (or even slaughtered for food consumption) on the same day.

Before beginning a lengthy discussion about the Jewish holidays, our reading teaches us about a very serious and difficult commandment. We are told that we must sanctify God's Name (called "kiddush Hashem" in Hebrew) by giving up our lives rather than violating any of the three most serious sins in Judaism: murder, idol worship, and being physically intimate with someone forbidden to us. This is a very complex area of Jewish law, and we are indeed blessed to live in times when people are not forced to make such difficult choices.

As for the holidays, our reading begins with a brief mention of the Sabbath, then turns to the holiday of Passover and the commandment to eat matzah. We find here the additional commandment to bring a barley offering (known as an "omer") on the second day of Passover. Following this offering is a seven-week counting period that ends when the holiday of Shavuot (Pentecost in English) begins. After discussing this holiday's Temple service, the reading briefly interrupts its discussion of the holidays to mention that farmers must, when harvesting their fields, leave certain parts of their fields unharvested for the poor.

The High Holidays—Rosh Hashanah (the Jewish New Year) and Yom Kippur (the Day of Atonement)—are also discussed here. We are specifically commanded to hear the shofar (ram's horn) on Rosh Hashanah and to "afflict" ourselves on Yom Kippur. After which, we read about Sukkot (Tabernacles in English). We are told that during this seven-day holiday, we must sit in outdoor booths, take the Four Species (citron, palm branch, myrtles, and willows), and be particularly joyful before God. The final holiday mentioned in this reading is Shemini Atzeret, a one-day celebration which immediately follows Sukkot.

Related to the holidays are instructions about the daily lighting of the Temple menorah, which can only be done with the purest of olive oils. We are also commanded about the twelve showbreads that must be arranged on a special golden table in the Mishkan every Shabbat.

Our reading concludes on a sad and harsh note, as we read the story of a Jewish man who was put to death for cursing God. This is followed by a listing of the penalties for committing murder, property damages, and personal injury.

Life Lessons from *Emor*

This week's reading has some commandments that people are usually familiar with, but many of these same people misunderstand what these commandments are really about. Let's see if we can set the record straight while we learn a few key life lessons.

One Should Never Be Cruel

As we have seen, Jewish law can be complicated. Some parts are easily understood, like the common-sense laws we have previously discussed. Others leave us completely mystified, as they seem to make no sense at all, like the prohibition against wearing a garment made with a mixture of wool and linen.

Sometimes confusion about Jewish law can become problematic. Consider the example of *shechita*, the method of ritual slaughtering used to prepare kosher meats. Several European countries—Switzerland, Sweden, Poland, and Norway—have banned *shechita* on the grounds that it is cruel to animals, crueler even than the methods used to slaughter non-kosher animals.

These bans reflect a deep misunderstanding not only of *shechita*, but of Jewish law generally.

Judaism strongly prohibits animal cruelty, especially causing animals unnecessary pain. There is even a special phrase for this in Hebrew: *tza'ar ba'alei chayim* (literally translated as "the pain inflicted upon living things). The first example of this prohibition found in the Torah appears early in the book of Genesis, where

God tells Noah and his descendants that, while they may eat meat, they may not tear a limb from a living animal.[2]

Based on this prohibition, later biblical and rabbinic law require that animals meant for human consumption be slaughtered as humanely as possible. That is what *shechita* is designed to do: kill the animal as quickly and as painlessly as possible with a single stroke of the knife. The great legal scholar Rabbi Moses Maimonides makes this point very clear:

> Since the desire of procuring good food necessitates the slaying of animals, the Torah commands that the death of the animal should be the easiest. It is not allowed to torment the animal by cutting the throat in a clumsy manner, by piercing it, or by cutting off a limb while the animal is still alive.[3]

Yes, Jews are permitted to eat meat, but they are commanded to take precautions to be sure that their desires for meat do not cause unnecessary suffering to animals. It should thus come as no surprise (and with all due respect to Switzerland, Sweden, Poland, and Norway) that *shechita* is generally understood to cause less suffering to animal than the methods typically used to slaughter non-kosher animals, many of which do not guarantee immediate death.[4]

There are other well-known commandments in the Torah against cruelty to animals. There is the prohibition against cooking

---

2. Genesis 9:3–4.

3. *Guide to the Perplexed* III:48.

4. In terms of non-kosher meat production, animal welfare advocates have found that most animals killed for food purposes, regardless of the conditions in which they were raised or bred, are often unnecessarily frightening and painful. See Kim, "Slaughterhouses."

a kid in its mother's milk.[5] Jews are also prohibited from taking eggs or chicks from a nest while the mother bird is present.[6] And in this week's reading, we are commanded not to slaughter a mother and her offspring on the same day.[7] What is common to these commandments is a concern for the emotional pain of the mother, who should neither see nor participate in the killing of her children.

You shouldn't be surprised by the Torah's concerns for the wellbeing of animals. The prohibitions against animal cruelty are meant to teach us several important life lessons.

First, they remind us that humans and animals alike are God's creatures. He watches over them both, and He helps both endure and thrive.

Second, we should not take God's handiwork for granted. This includes not needlessly slaughtering His creatures.

Lastly, these prohibitions are meant to keep us from becoming mean-spirited and to teach us to be merciful. This is why when the Torah does allow us to kill animals in certain circumstances, it tells us that it must be done with sensitivity. Killing a mother and her child on the same day, something specifically prohibited in this week's ready, would be needlessly cruel and is therefore forbidden.

Do you (or any of your friends) have pets? What kinds of things have you learned by taking care of your pet? Is being kind and merciful one of the lessons you've learned? How so?

One Should Never Understand This Literally

The following verses from this week's reading are even more misunderstood than Judaism's perspective on animal cruelty.

If any party maims another [person]: what was done shall be done in return—fracture for fracture, eye for eye,

5. Exodus 23:19.

6. Deuteronomy 22:6.

7. Leviticus 22:28.

tooth for tooth. The injury inflicted on a human being shall be inflicted in return.[8]

If you read these verses literally, they are saying that if you were to accidently break a friend's arm or, God forbid, poke out an eye, your friend could do the same to you. But that's crazy, isn't it?

Yes, it is, which is why the Jewish tradition has never read these verses literally. So, how are we to understand this commandment of "an eye for an eye?" The Talmudic sages give us a straightforward answer:

> It **is taught** in **another** *baraita* that **Rabbi Shimon ben Yoḥai says: "An eye for an eye"** (Leviticus 24:20), is referring to **monetary restitution.** Do **you say** that this is referring to **monetary restitution, or is it only** teaching that the one who caused the injury must lose **an actual eye?** There may be a case where **there was a blind person and he blinded** another, or there was **one with a severed limb and he severed** the limb of another, or there was **a lame person and he caused** another **to be lame. In this** case, **how can I fulfill "an eye for an eye"** literally, when he is already lacking the limb that must be injured? If one will suggest that in that case, a monetary penalty will be imposed, that can be refuted: **But the Torah stated: "You shall have one manner of law"** (Leviticus 24:22), which teaches that **the law** shall be **equal for all of you.**[9]

8. Leviticus 24:19—20.

9. Bava Kama 84a.

This is but one example from the Talmud in which the sages were insistent that these verses could not be read literally. The sages argued that taking the verses literally was simply impractical. (How could you take the eye of a blind man?) They also argued that a literal understanding of the verses would result in unfair or disproportionate punishments (as in, he might die). But perhaps the sages simply could not imagine worshipping a God so cruel that He would command such a thing.[10]

In the end, the Talmud and all later legal codes agreed that the idea of "eye for eye" was never to be taken literally. Instead, based on Judaism's oral tradition, these sources understood this commandment as requiring financial payments when a person harms another.[11] If that's the case, why would these verses be written in a way which could easily be read as requiring Jewish courts to cause terrible pain to people on a regular basis?

Here is one answer to think about.

We all know that people accused of breaking the law must appear in court where a judge or a jury will consider the facts and determine if the person is guilty or not. The laws are known to all, as are the rules the court must follow. In our example, where someone physically hurts a friend, the court decides whether that person was careful enough or whether there was just nothing this person could have done to avoid hurting the friend. The court

10. It is worth noting that in ancient Babylonia, their legal code, called the Hammurabi Code, used similar language. (Some secular scholars believe that many of the Torah's laws are derived from this Babylonian legal code.) That code used the words "an eye for an eye" literally, meaning, if you broke another person's arm, that person could break your arm in return. If you put out your friend's eye, that person could put out your eye. More shockingly, the Hammurabi Code mandated that if a goring ox killed a man, the owner of the ox (not the animal!) was put to death. If, however, the ox killed the son or daughter of another man, the owner's own son or daughter would be ordered killed in retribution. See Hertz, "Code of Hammurabi," 406.

11. As discussed at length in the Talmudic tractate Bava Kama, there are five separate categories of damages to be paid: (i) for the harm or injury itself; (ii) for pain and suffering; (iii) to cover medical expenses; (iv) to cover any lost wages should the injured party be unable to work; and (v) for the embarrassment the injured party suffers because of the damages inflicted upon him or her.

would then decide what the person owes the friend in terms of financial repayment. Ten dollars? A thousand dollars? A million dollars? That's up to the court if the judge and jury determine that the person was at fault.

Now imagine there is a Heavenly court where God sits in judgment. God knows the true facts in a way that a judge and jury cannot. God knows with certainty if the person deserves the same hurt that the friend suffered, be it a broken arm or a lost eye. This is why the verses read as if the person should be punished with "an eye for an eye." Money alone cannot make up for the harm the person did. Something else must be done, but inflicting the same harm on the person, especially if it was accident, would be cruel and unreasonable. What then is the verse hinting at with the phrase "an eye for an eye?" Quite simply, that the one who causes harm must beg forgiveness from the one who was harmed.

Some injuries are not so bad and heal quickly. Others never heal, and the person who was hurt is never made whole again. But forgiveness sincerely asked for and sincerely given can, in the eyes of the Heavenly court, do a great deal to undo the damage. That is the critical life lesson to be learned from "an eye for an eye."

> *Can you think of a time when a friend hurt you (accidently or otherwise)? What did you do when your friend apologized? Did you accept the apology? Did that make you feel better? A little? A lot?*
>
> *And if you did not accept the apology, how did that make you feel? Better or worse?*

NNN

Behar

(Leviticus 25:1—26:2)

Summary of This Week's Reading

Our reading this week begins with two related commandments: the Shmita (Sabbatical) and Jubilee years. Let's start with Shmita. Every seventh year is a Shmita year, during which no farming is done in the Land of Israel. (If letting the land rest every seven years reminds you of the Sabbath, good for you. Now you understand why it's called the "Sabbatical Year.") Even though we may not work the land, any fruit or vegetables that grow on their own are considered ownerless and may be harvested by anyone.

The Jubilee year is connected to but is distinct from the Shmita years.

After seven sets of seven years, a Jubilee year is proclaimed by a blast of the shofar (ram's horn) on that year's Yom Kippur (Day of Atonement). During Jubilee years, all the laws of the Shmita year apply, and, in addition to these laws, all slaves are set free, all lands revert to their original owners, and all debts are to be forgiven.

Our reading goes on to spell out exactly how lands are to revert to their original owners. The total price for which the land was sold is divided by the number of years from the time of purchase until the next Jubilee year (when the land would automatically return to the owner) to determine the price per year. The original owner then re-funds the buyer however much money he had paid for the remaining years. What's more, a person who sells real-estate has the option of "redeeming" the land from the purchaser—provided that two years have passed from the date of purchase. A relative of the seller may also redeem the land on behalf of his family member.

There's more still on this topic.

All the laws involved the sale of land apply to fields and homes in un-walled cities. Homes in walled cities may be redeemed for their full value for up to one year after the sale. If not redeemed within the year, they become the permanent property of the buyer, and they are not released by the Jubilee. Another exception to these rules is the property allotted to the Levites. The homes and fields in the forty-eight Levite cities are always redeemable—from the moment of purchase until the Jubilee year, when they again revert to their owners.

An obvious concern regarding the Shmita years is this: "What will we eat in the seventh year if we do not farm or harvest our crops?" God reassures the people that He will bless the sixth year's harvest so that it will produce enough to provide for three years: year six, year seven (the Shmita year), and year eight (until that year's crops are ready to eat). Moses then explains why land may not be sold forever but may only be "leased" until the Jubilee year. It is as God says: "the land is Mine; you are but a stranger resident with Me."

Next comes a series of commandments that touch on looking out for others in times of need. For example, there is the commandment to assist other Jews by coming to their aid before they become financially ruined and dependent on the help of others. Another commandment prohibits Jews from charging interest on a loan to a fellow Jew.

Our reading concludes with a brief mention of the prohibition against idolatry and the requirement to observe the Shabbat and revere the Holy Sanctuary.

Life Lessons from *Behar*

This week's reading has some unexpected life lessons about how people should do business. Who knew that a book that spends so much time discussing sacrifices would have so much to say about this topic?

Putting Things into Perspective

We live in truly wondrous times. Men have walked on the moon, and we have sent space probes to the farthest reaches of our solar system and beyond. You and your family could literally get on an airplane and fly to just about anywhere in the world and be there in less than a day. You can log onto your computer and get more information than you can process on any topic you choose in a matter of seconds. People live longer than ever and reach ages unimaginable a generation or two ago.[1] Doctors today almost routinely perform heart, lung, and liver transplants. Medical researchers are even experimenting with mind-controlled robotic limbs which, when perfected, will allow patients with amputations, traumatic injuries, or who were born without a limb to utilize a complete and full range of motion.[2]

And let's not get started on all the things you can do, be they important or trivial, with a cell phone.

What's interesting about all this is that you are probably unaware of how special the times you are living in really are. How could you? Things that might have seemed to have come straight out of a science fiction movie to your grandparents and perhaps even to your parents are part of your everyday life.

While the Torah does not deal with things like cell phones and the internet, it does recognize how hard it can be for people to put their lives into perspective. That is, the Torah recognizes that people may not realize how good they have it or how much better things are for them than they were for their parents and grandparents. The Torah therefore has a mechanism for helping us gain perspective. It's called "shmita." Here's how it's described in this week's Torah reading:

> When you enter the land that I assign to you, the land
> shall observe a sabbath of God. Six years you may sow

---

1. There are more than 97,000 people in the US who are 100 years old or more. While this represents a small percentage of total population, it is still a remarkable figure.

2. Gohd, "Advanced Mind-Controlled Robotic Arm."

> your field, and six years you may prune your vineyard
> and gather in the yield. But in the seventh year the land
> shall have a sabbath of complete rest, a sabbath of God:
> you shall not sow your field or prune your vineyard. You
> shall not reap the aftergrowth of your harvest or gather
> the grapes of your untrimmed vines; it shall be a year of
> complete rest for the land.[3]

When the commandment to observe shmita was first given, most of the Jewish people were farmers. So, if they did not farm during the seventh year, what were they to do? The simplest answer would be to refocus and reset their priorities. During the shmita year, they would have a chance to deepen their connection with God because shmita gave them an opportunity to pray and study without the distraction of having to rush out to tend their fields. They would have more time for their spouses and children, too. In other words, they would remember that there could be more to life than their daily chores. God's plan was that they might realize all they had to be thankful for and have the time to enjoy life.

Of course, not farming during the seventh year required great trust in God. After all, if they did not farm, what would they eat? In those days, if you did not farm, you had nothing to eat!

The sad truth is that the people's faith was not as strong as it should have been. In the end, they did not properly observe the shmita year. Not once, but seventy times, and according to the Book of Chronicles, this is why the exile to Babylonia (which occurred after the destruction of the First Temple) lasted seventy years: one year of exile to make up for each year shmita was not observed.[4]

Today, almost none of us are farmers, and even if we were, shmita must only be observed in the land of Israel and only when

---

3. Leviticus 25:2–5.

4. "Those who survived the sword he exiled to Babylon, and they became his and his sons' servants till the rise of the Persian kingdom, in fulfillment of the word of the LORD spoken by Jeremiah, until the land paid back its sabbaths; as long as it lay desolate it kept sabbath, till seventy years were completed." (II Chronicles 36:21)

most Jews are living in the land of Israel.[5] But don't think that shmita is no longer relevant. While we don't actually observe shmita, the idea of it can still remind us of how important it is to take time on a regular basis to refocus and reset our priorities. You need not wait seven years to do so, nor must you spend an entire year on it, but keeping your life in perspective is something all of us would benefit from.

> *Having a day of rest like the Sabbath every week is a good way to help people refocus and reset their priorities. How does the Sabbath help you and your family do this? Do you find it helpful? Important?*

The Problem with Charging Interest

Your family most likely owns a car, maybe even two. And there's a good chance your family owns the house you live in (although not every family is fortunate enough to own their own home).[6]

When your parents were ready to buy a car or the house you live in, one of the first things they probably did was speak to a bank about borrowing money. The same is true for businesses, both large and small. When they need to build new factories to produce more of whatever they sell or when they need to invest in new equipment to help grow their businesses, they, too, turn to banks to borrow money.

Modern economies are all based on the idea that people and businesses can easily borrow money. History shows us that when

5. There are some in the modern State of Israel who continue to observe shmita. (Since the establishment of Israel in 1948, shmita has been observed in 1951–52, 1958–59, 1965–66, 1972–73, 1979–80, 1986–87, 1993–94, 2000–1, 2007–8, 2014–15, and 2021–22.) Those who do observe shmita laws refrain from eating any fruits or vegetables grown by Jews in Israel. Instead, they rely on produce grown by non-Jewish Arabs or produce imported from other countries. Additionally, while the debt forgiveness aspect of the shmita is relatively forgotten, courts will still honor the annulment of debt if both parties agree.

6. According to data from the US Census Bureau, about two-thirds of Americans own their own home.

loans are available, people can start new businesses and bring new ideas and inventions to the market. Existing businesses make higher profits. Builders can build bigger and more modern homes and factories. More families can live in better homes.

Sounds good for everyone, right? But what about the banks? Why do they lend money to people and businesses? The answer is simple. They make money by lending money. Here's how it works.

Let's say your parents need to borrow $1,000 to buy a new car. They ask the bank for a loan, and once the bank is sure that your parents will be able to repay the loan, the bank gives them the money. The bank also tells them how long they have to pay back the money.

To keep things simple, let's assume that the bank gives your parents one year to pay off their loan. The bank will also add one more important condition, which is the interest rate your parents will pay on the money they borrow. In our example, let's assume that the interest rate is ten percent. This means that at the end of the year, your parents will repay the bank $1,100,  that is, the $1,000 they borrowed (which we call the principal) plus the interest owed on the money they borrowed, which totals $100 in our example.

At this point, perhaps you are wondering what all this has to do with our weekly Torah reading. Our readings are usually about commandments, not lessons in business. A quick look at the text of our reading gives us this answer:

> If your kin (אָחִיךָ), being in straits, come under your authority, and are held by you as though resident aliens, let them live by your side: do not exact advance or accrued interest, but fear your God. Let your kin (אָחִיךָ) live by your side as such. Do not lend your money at advance

interest, nor give your food at accrued interest. I Hashem
am your God, who brought you out of the land of Egypt,
to give you the land of Canaan, to be your God.[7]

Seems strange, doesn't it? If lending money helps people, and banks lend money because they can charge interest, why does God tell the Jewish people that they cannot charge interest on the money they lend to one another? What's even stranger is that a Jew is permitted to borrow money from non-Jews and pay interest to them. A Jew is also permitted to lend money to non-Jews and collect interest from them (just as non-Jews are permitted to lend and borrow money to and from each other with interest).

Why should there be a difference between Jews and non-Jews when it comes to lending money? After all, the Torah makes no distinction between Jews and non-Jews when it warns us against theft and fraud and other matters related to business.

Part of the answer is that theft and fraud involve one person cheating another. There is never an excuse for cheating someone else, and therefore the Torah treats everyone equally. With charging interest on a loan, both parties (the lender and the borrower) agree to this up front. So maybe there is room to treat Jews and non-Jews differently. But this does not help us understand why God chooses to do so.

The real answer is found in the verses themselves. The verses we quoted use the word "kin" when prohibiting interest. ("Kin" is a loose translation. The actual Hebrew word used in the verses means "your brother.") The Torah prohibits interest between Jews because a fellow Jew is family (even when he is not literally your brother, and she is not literally your sister). Family members ought to help one another, especially in hard times, simply because they are family. Lending money to a family member in need is a very good and praiseworthy thing. Lending money to them and charging interest cannot be considered "help." It's you making money off of their problems.

7. Leviticus 25:35–38.

When God tells the Jewish people that they cannot charge interest on money they lend to one another, He is reminding them that the Jewish nation is meant to behave like a family. In other words, God expects each of us to be concerned for another's benefit as much as we are concerned with our own.

> *Can you think of other things you or your family do that reminds you that the Jewish people are like one big family? What is it about these things that makes you think of family?*

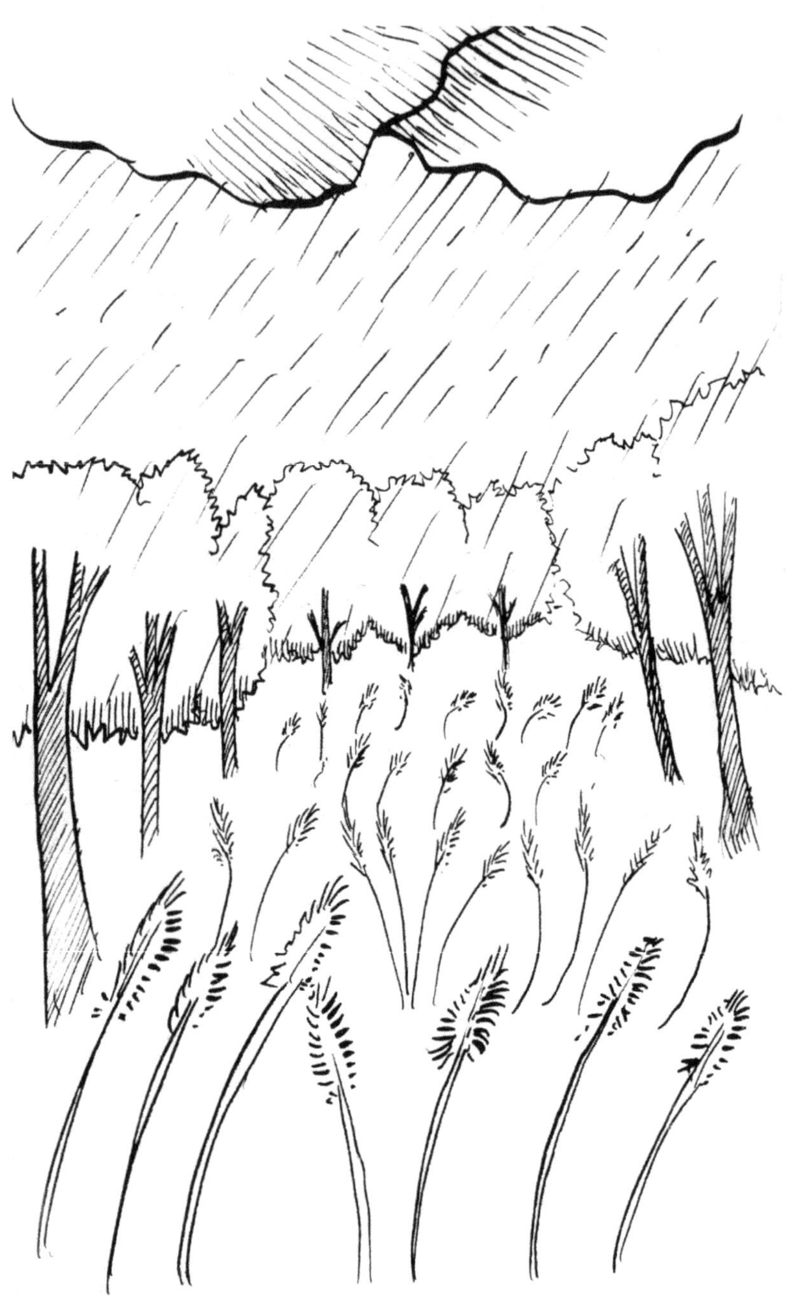

Bechukotai

(Leviticus 26:3—27:34)

Summary of This Week's Reading

This week's reading contains a striking description of the rewards for observing God's commandments and the series of punishments that will befall the Jewish people if they choose to disregard them. For example, Jews are promised incredible blessing if they diligently study Torah and observe God's commandments. The blessings include plentiful food, timely rain, peace in the land, the elimination of wild animals from the land, incredible military success, and an overabundance of crops. Best of all, God's presence will be revealed among the people.

Then comes a description of the terrifying punishments which will befall the Jews if they reject God's commandments. The punishments include disease, famine, enemy occupation of the land, exile, and desolation of the land. The non-observance of the Sabbatical year is singled out as the reason for the desolation of the land. (We will return to this in greater detail below.)

Our reading next turns to a new topic: promises one makes about gifts or sacrifices to be brought to the Temple. A person can pledge the worth of an individual, in which case the Torah tells us how much the person must pay. (It all depends on the gender and age of the individual who is being "assessed.") An animal that is pledged to the Temple must be offered on the altar if it is fit for sacrifice— otherwise it must be "redeemed" for its value. If the owner chooses to redeem it, he or she must add one fifth of its value to the redemption price. The same rule applies to a house that is pledged to the Temple.

There are also special rules when one promises to give land to the Temple. If it is land that was part of the family lot (given to his ancestors when Israel was divided amongst the Tribes), the redemption price is a fixed amount, depending on its harvest yield. If the owner chooses not to redeem it, it may be redeemed by any other individual. In this event, or if the land remains un-redeemed, the land becomes the property of the priests during the next Jubilee year. On a related note, we learn that land that was purchased and then consecrated by the buyer can also be redeemed, but it reverts to its original owner when the Jubilee arrives.

There are additional laws regarding things that are automatically considered to belong to the Temple, such as all firstborn livestock. These are sacrificed in the Temple, and their flesh is consumed by the priests. (A person also has the option of dedicating and consecrating any of his belongings specifically for the use of the priests.)

Another example of something that is automatically connected to the Temple is the "Second Tithe." This, we are told, must be consumed by its owners in Jerusalem. However, if it is too burdensome to bring to Jerusalem, it can be redeemed by its owner. We also read about the animal tithe—every tenth animal is offered as a sacrifice, and the meat consumed by its owners. With this, we conclude the Book of Leviticus.

Life Lessons from *Bechukotai*

It's always important to carefully read the words and verse in each weekly reading. This week, however, it's particularly important to do so because, if you don't, you could miss some very valuable life lessons.

When is a Reward Not a Reward?

At first glance, the beginning of this week's reading is confusing.

> If you follow My laws and faithfully observe My com-
> mandments, I will grant your rains in their season, so that
> the earth shall yield its produce and the trees of the field
> their fruit. Your threshing shall overtake the vintage, and
> your vintage shall overtake the sowing; you shall eat your
> fill of bread and dwell securely in your land. I will grant
> peace in the land, and you shall lie down untroubled by
> anyone; I will give the land respite from vicious beasts,
> and no sword shall cross your land.[1]

These verses seem quite clear in stating that if the Jewish people follow God's commandments, He will reward them greatly: with rain in its proper time, abundant crops, and peace with their enemies and any wild beasts that roam the land of Israel. One cannot help but feel excited when reading these verses. After all, who doesn't like being rewarded for their actions?

There is, however, one big problem with all this. The rabbinic tradition insists that we should not keep God's commandments for the sake of a reward. Rather, we should simply do them, just as a servant simply follows the orders of his or her ruler (king or queen, it makes no difference).[2]

How do we resolve this contradiction?

There is a beautiful Hassidic answer to this problem. It turns out that this week's reading is not the only one that suggests God will reward the Jewish people if they follow his commandments. For example, in the book of Deuteronomy, in the reading of Ekev, we find a promise very similar to that found in this week's reading:

> And if you do obey these rules and observe them care-
> fully, your God Hashem will maintain faithfully for you
> the covenant made on oath with your fathers: [God] will
> favor you and bless you and multiply you—blessing your
> issue from the womb and your produce from the soil,
> your new grain and wine and oil, the calving of your herd
> and the lambing of your flock, in the land sworn to your

1. Leviticus 26:3–6.

2. See Avot 1:3, where the Mishnah states: "Do not be like servants who serve the master in the expectation of receiving a reward but be like servants who serve the master without the expectation of receiving a reward."

> fathers to be assigned to you. You shall be blessed above
> all other peoples: there shall be no sterile male or female
> among you or among your livestock.[3]

Again, a simple reading of the verses seems to say that there are great rewards for keeping God's commandments. And again, this contradicts the idea that we should serve God simply because He is God, with no expectation of a reward.

The Hassidic answer to the problem requires that we reread the verses very carefully. What are the so-called rewards listed in both examples? Everyday things, like rain when it's needed. Success in growing crops and raising livestock (something that in our time would be more like having a well-paying job or a profitable business). Peaceful times so that people can enjoy the good that God bestows upon them.

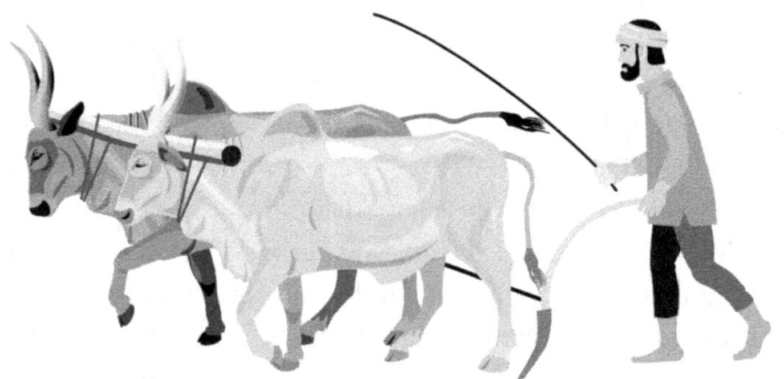

What's missing from this list? A promise of eternal life in the World to Come, which Judaism considers the ultimate reward for serving God. Whatever the World to Come might be, it is not something we can see or touch.[4] We would call it a spiritual, not a tangible (or real) reward.

3. Deuteronomy 7:12–14.

4. While there is much discussion in Jewish sources about the World to Come, there is little agreement on what it is. However, all agree that it most certainly is not like heaven as portrayed in movies and children's books. There are no angels with halos and harps floating on clouds in the Jewish World to Come.

This is an important difference, and this, say the Hassidim, explains the problem with the promise of a reward in the beginning of our reading. The rain and crops and peace God promises for keeping His commandments should not be thought of as rewards. Rather, they are signals from God that we can see and feel. They are meant to tell us that we are doing good and that we should continue doing what we've been doing. It is as if God is patting us on the back for a job well done (or maybe putting a gold star on a chore chart He might have for us).

In a sense, these signals are more important than rewards. A reward suggests that we've finished the task before us and that there is nothing left for us to do or accomplish. But in life, there is always something for us to accomplish, and there are always God's commandments to follow. Signs from God that let us know we're on the right track are thus very important because they can (and should) motivate us to continue on the proper life paths we've chosen.

> *How do your parents or teachers let you know that you've done something well? Does this make you want to keep at it or even find other things you can do for them?*

People of the Book

For centuries, Jews have been referred to as "the people of the book." Historically, the term originates from Islam, whose followers recognize that other people and other religions possess written revelations from God that preceded the Koran, the Islamic bible.

For the Jews, the "book" is, of course, the Torah and, by extension, the many books associated with it, such as the Talmud, commentaries, and codes of Jewish law. These not only define Jewish law. They are the touchstone[5] of Jewish life and Jewish culture.

---

5. A touchstone is the standard or criterion by which something is judged or recognized.

A defining characteristic of Jews as a people of the book has always been the emphasis Jewish families place on education and knowledge. In every era and in every country in which Jews have found themselves, Jewish parents have stressed the importance of a good education to their children. (Just stop for a moment and ask yourself, is this true in your family? Was it true for your parents when they were growing up?)

There's a hint to all this at the end of this week's reading. It may not be obvious at first glance, so let's dig a little deeper.

Our reading (as well as the book of Leviticus) concludes with a brief discussion of the "Second Tithe" (called *Maaser Sheni* in Hebrew). The Torah tells us that *Maaser Sheni* must be taken from all grains, wine, and oil grown in Israel.[6] The total was to be ten percent of each type of item, and these were set aside and kept in a state of ritual purity. What's more, *Maaser Sheni* produce could only be eaten by people who were in a similar state of purity. Finally, the produce could be eaten at any time during the year, but only in Jerusalem.[7]

---

6. The Talmudic sages extended this to include fruits and vegetables.

7. God is nothing if not practical. If the distance to Jerusalem was too great or if it was simply too difficult to transport the grains and oils to Jerusalem, the Torah allows a person to exchange these things for money (Deuteronomy

This all seems very complicated. Why would the Torah insist that people go to Jerusalem to eat the food they set aside as *Maaser Sheni*?

A beautiful answer is found in a book called *Sefer HaChinuch*.[8] It tells us that in the times of the Temple, the average person did not have a lot of time to learn Torah. This is understandable, because being a farmer in those days was a hard and demanding job. Farmers worked long hours every day (except for the Sabbath), and this left them with little time (and probably little energy) for Torah study. The obligation to bring *Maaser Sheni* to Jerusalem gave farmers a break from their hard work. They would find themselves in Jerusalem, a center of Torah learning and the place where the great Sanhedrin sat and issued important rulings in Jewish law. Since at least one member from each household made this pilgrimage to Jerusalem each year, this, says the *Sefer HaChinuch*, ensured that every Jewish home would have at least one Torah scholar.

Today, there is no Temple and thus no obligation to bring *Maaser Sheni* to Jerusalem. But the desire that Jewish families have that their children be well-educated, perhaps maybe even great scholars, remains as strong as it was in ancient times.

What do your parents do to show you how important a
good education is? Are you convinced yet?

14:24). This money would then be brought to Jerusalem where it must be used to buy food to be eaten in the Holy City. The Torah further states that when exchanging the food for money, one would have to add a "redemption fee" of an extra twenty-five percent (Leviticus 27:30).

8. The book's title literally means "Book of Education" and it systematically discusses the 613 commandments of the Torah. Published anonymously in thirteenth-century Spain, the book discusses each commandment, both from a legal and a moral perspective. It then presents a brief overview of the practical Jewish law governing each commandment and closes with a summary as to the commandment's applicability in our time.

About the Author

Rabbi Reuven Travis earned his bachelor's degree from Dartmouth College, where he graduated Phi Beta Kappa, with a double major in French literature and political science. He holds a master's degree in teaching from Mercer University and earned a master's in Judaic studies from Spertus College. He received his rabbinic ordination from Rabbi Michael J. Broyde, dean of the Atlanta Torah MiTzion Kollel, after spending four years studying with Rabbi Broyde and members of the kollel.

Rabbi Travis worked in Jewish day schools for twenty years and taught students from second grade through high school. In addition to this *Curious Student's Guide* series, he has also published scholarly works on the books of Job, Genesis, Exodus, and Numbers, respectively, and is currently working on several new book projects. He also teaches online classes on topics ranging from the Bible to Jewish medical ethics and American history.

Bibliography

"Animal Sacrifice? Really?" 2017. https://bibleproject.com/blog/animal-sacrifice-really/.

Enns, Pete. "Why Rituals Are Really Really Important for Your Faith." https://peteenns.com/rituals-really-really-important-faith/.

Duyndam, Joachim, et al. "Sacrifice in Modernity: Community, Ritual, Identity." In *Sacrifice in Modernity: Community, Ritual, Identity: From Nationalism and Nonviolence to Health Care and Harry Potter*, edited by Joachim Duyndam et al., 3–14. Leiden: Brill, 2017. https://doi.org/10.1163/9789004335530_002.

Gohd, Chelsea. "Florida Man Becomes First Person to Live with Advanced Mind-Controlled Robotic Arm." Feb 3, 2018. https://futurism.com/mind-controlled-robotic-arm-johnny-matheny.

Hertz, Rabbi J. H. "Is the Code of Hammurabi the Source of the Mosaic Civil Law?" In *The Pentateuch and Haftorahs, Second Edition*. London: Soncino Press, 1963.

Kim, Hemi. "Slaughterhouses: The Harsh Reality of How Meat Is Made." Jul 1, 2022. https://sentientmedia.org/slaughterhouses/.

Kirzane, Daniel. "Understanding Biblical Sacrifice (Korbanot): What Sacrifice Is, Where It Comes From, and What It Can Mean for Us Today." https://www.myjewishlearning.com/article/understanding-biblical-sacrifice-korbanot/.

Morinis, Alan. "Reading for Gratitude, *Hakarat haTov* / Gratitude." https://jewishcamp.org/wp-content/uploads/sites/5/2017/04/Gratitude_-_Mussar_Institute.pdf.

Nahmanides. *The Disputation at Barcelona: Ramban: Nahmanides*. Translated by Charles B Chavel. Hawthorne: BN Publishing, 2017.

Reed, Annette Y. "From Sacrifice to the Slaughterhouse: Ancient and Modern Perspectives on Meat, Ritual, and Civilization." *Method & Theory in the Study of Religion* 26.2 (2014) 111–58.

Bibliography

"Sevens Reasons Why Seeking Revenge Is a Bad Idea." Sep 14, 2022. https://www.ditchthelabel.org/7-reasons-revenge-is-a-bad-idea/.

Tanakh: A New Translation of the Holy Scriptures according to the Traditional Hebrew Text. Philadelphia: Jewish Publication Society, 1985.

www.ingramcontent.com/pod-product-compliance
Lightning Source LLC
Chambersburg PA
CBHW070738030726
47601CB00001B/56